# Gourmet Coffee Owner's Manual

## Includes the secrets to making perfect espresso at home

By

Nancy Faubel

authorHOUSE™

1663 LIBERTY DRIVE, SUITE 200
BLOOMINGTON, INDIANA 47403
(800) 839-8640
WWW.AUTHORHOUSE.COM

*First published by AuthorHouse 01/31/05*

*ISBN: 1-4208-0805-2 (sc)*

*Printed in the United States of America*
*Bloomington, Indiana*

*This book is printed on acid-free paper.*

# Dedication

This book is dedicated to all those involved in the growing, production, processing, and consumption of coffee, the world's favorite beverage!

# Author's comments

This book actually came about because of something that happened early on in my coffee career. So, I'd like to share this story with you: a story about losing not only a sale for a top-of-the-line $800.00 home espresso machine but also of losing a faithful daily customer as a result of what I'm about to share with you. On the surface, that doesn't sound very good, but read on...

One of my best espresso-loving customers used to come in to the shop every day for one of our famous espresso drinks, and one day he was looking at a big $800.00 espresso machine that he was thinking of buying to make the drinks at home. As I started to explain the features, he told me he knew the concepts because he already owned a $70.00 home espresso machine, but that it didn't work right because the espresso was awful. After asking him a few questions about what he was doing, I was able to give him a few suggestions, and he went home to try it with the machine he already had.

I didn't see him again for several weeks, and when I did finally did run across him and asked him where he'd been, he told me he went home and tried my suggestions, and it turned out that the machine he already had could actually make perfect espresso (there went my $800.00 sale!). Then he said that because the machine did such a great job, he was making his own espresso every morning instead of coming into the shop, so that cost me not only the $800.00 sale, but a daily customer as well!

Eventually, through dealing with the public on a daily basis, I became aware of the fact that there was a lot of misinformation circulating about coffee, the different coffee drinks, the different kinds of coffee, different roasts, etc., that prevented people from really getting maximum enjoyment from this centuries-old beverage. My library and bookstore research yielded books that were historical, technical, or coffee cookbooks, but there wasn't really anything out there that addressed the basic concepts about coffee and its preparation.

This book was written to share information that will allow the reader to get maximum enjoyment from the beverage and the ritual that is coffee. Hopefully, the hints and techniques outlined in this book will help the reader produce superior coffee drinks at home and continue to enjoy the flavors and nuances of this wonderful beverage!

# Introduction

This manual is written to give you, the Gourmet Coffee Owner, an overview of coffee. The goal is to answer your coffee questions, clear up common misunderstandings about coffee and preparation methods, and give you some ideas on ways to use coffee in recipes and specialty drinks. These topics cover most of the questions I've been asked in the many years I've spent in the coffee business.

With a better understanding of the basics of coffee and how to prepare it, you can enjoy gourmet coffee to the fullest. The best coffee in the world can be rendered unpalatable by incorrect storage, the wrong grind, and improper preparation. Conversely, it is not necessary to spend $7,000.00 to get a perfect shot of espresso. A minimal investment in coffee equipment that will last a lifetime is all that is required. Of course, the equipment has to be used properly to achieve the desired result, something that this book covers in detail.

We've tried to make this book contain information of interest to the coffee aficionado in sufficient detail to be workable and interesting, without being boring or going into too much detail. For detailed information, we refer our readers to www.coffeeresearch. org, which actually goes into the chemistry of coffee, and gives a highly technical explanation of various coffees and processes.

There are all different grades and types of coffee, ranging in price from Robusta at $1.50 per pound to the finest Estate coffees at $60-75 per pound. (Most of the Estate coffee winds up in Europe and Japan, though.) Although $60-75 might seem like a lot to spend for coffee, it's actually a good value, because unlike a $60 bottle of wine which is consumed in one evening, a $60 bag of coffee will last a month or two. Put another way, a glass of $60 wine is $15.00, and a cup of $60.00 coffee is 75 cents.

We're going to cover everything from the origin of coffee to how it is processed, how it is graded, how it is roasted, how it is flavored, and how it is decaffeinated. What grind works best with what equipment and why, what temperature is best to produce that perfect cup, and what coffee to select depending on the flavor profile you prefer. And, last but not least, a whole chapter dedicated to showing you how to make perfect espresso at home with a $70.00 home espresso machine!

Let's get started!

*Nancy Faubel*

# Table of Contents

# Chapter One The History of Coffee

Coffee originated in Ethiopia, a country in the northeastern area of Africa. The original story goes that a sheepherder noticed his sheep getting more energetic from eating the berries off the ol' coffee plant, and thus coffee was born.

It's my considered opinion, however, that sheep and goats, not being too expressive, are not the ones to place this idea in our young sheepherder's mind. A closer analysis immediately reveals the fact that this chosen goat herder, nameless but a legend nonetheless, was actually lamenting the absence of a nearby McDonalds, and started nibbling the soon-to-be-famous beans himself. He enjoyed his caffeine buzz and being much more articulate than his goats, rushed in to town with the news. Herds of villagers immediately returned to the site of this miracle plant, identified it, and the more entrepreneurial villagers soon figured out how to sell it and make some money, or a "Buck," an entrepreneurial effort that really exploded in the mid 80s with the coffee giant who bears its name, although the Buck long ago turned plural, as in "Bucks."

Anyway, coffee still grows wild in Ethiopia, but it was in Yemen that coffee was first cultivated. Although there is some disagreement as to the beginnings of cultivated coffee, by the 15th century it was certainly established. Yemen was one of the busiest countries in the world at the time, and its main port, Mocha, was one of the main centers of civilization. It was in Mocha that the first coffee houses were established as gathering places.

Coffee began its movement along the same latitudes as it was first cultivated, expanding to India and Sri Lanka (formerly Ceylon). During the early 17th century, coffee spread to the colonies of European countries, from Malabar (India) to Java (Indonesia). In the early 18th century, coffee made its way to South and Central America and the Caribbean. Now, coffee is grown in most subtropical countries, including most of Central and South America, the Caribbean, Africa, the Middle East, Asia, Australia, and the Pacific Rim. Contrary to popular belief, coffee is not grown in Europe. French Roast coffee is not grown in France, and Italian coffee is not grown in Italy. The names have to do with the roasts, not the origins. In fact, most "European-style" coffees originate in Africa and Indonesia. These coffee beans produce a stronger and fuller bodied brewed coffee.

Many regions around the world have retained their particular method of drinking coffee, much like the Japanese and their tea ceremonies. Turkish coffee, for example, is made by boiling coffee that has been ground almost to a powder. Then there's French Press coffee, which is coarsely ground and extracted through a French Press, American-style drip-brewed coffee, and of course the most famous of them all, espresso!

Coffee beans are actually the seeds of the coffee plant. When processed to remove their outer shell (cherry) and husk, they become the coffee bean known to coffee lovers. Most coffee beans are easily split into two comparatively large flat halves; peaberries are a special type of small round bean with only one part. Peaberries grow that way, and are generally sorted out of specialty grade coffee. This is because their smaller size would throw off the roast, as they would burn before the larger beans were finished roasting. Because of their interesting shape and intense flavor, they are frequently sold as a strictly peaberry blend, such as Tanzania Peaberry or Hawaiian Peaberry.

Whether it is espresso, cappuccino, or just a plain cup of java, the fresher the coffee, the better! As coffee ages, it loses aromatics, which are an important component of the coffee. In fact, the smell of things we eat and drink is often what we really think we "taste!" As coffee continues to age after it is roasted, there are chemical changes as well, including oxidation of the beans. The oils on the beans will actually go rancid after enough time has passed, which decidedly affects the flavor of coffee. When coffee gets more than two or three months old, it is so stale that it has lost almost all its flavor. Contrary to popular belief, freezing coffee does not extend its life, just like it doesn't extend the life of fresh bread. Freezing food mainly prevents deterioration from bacteria and molds, and does nothing to preserve freshness, anyone who has tasted freezer burned food can attest!

With fresh coffee, properly stored and properly prepared, delicious beverages can be created. New recipes are constantly being created to enhance the flavor of coffee, especially for the ubiquitous lattes and mochas. With some care, most of these drinks can be successfully made at home, with a minimal investment in equipment, as will be explained further into this book. It is not necessary to have a $7,000.00 commercial grade espresso machine to make a perfect shot of espresso to use in your favorite coffee drink.

When you choose to enjoy this wonderful beverage, you can contemplate the mystique and rich history that surrounds it. Coffee is actually one of the largest traded commodities in the world, and literally millions of people make their living in bringing it to you. Its production requires growers, exporters, ocean freighters, importers, roasters, consulting companies, independent certifying agencies (for organic coffee and Fair Trade® coffee), bag manufacturers, roaster manufacturers, coffee brewing equipment manufacturers, filter manufacturers, transportation companies, futures traders and brokers, grading and quality overseers, and that's just for the coffee! Then there are syrup manufacturers, chocolate producers, cup manufacturers, all range of dairy operations, and the coffee shops themselves.

So, when you enjoy a cup of coffee, no matter how it was produced or where it was grown, you're partaking in a tradition that has been around for centuries and contributing to a livelihood that has existed for centuries!

# Chapter Two Coffee's Journey from Plant to Cup

C offee is grown primarily in regions of the world between the Tropic of Cancer and the Tropic of Capricorn. Coffee just won't grow in other regions. Although coffee can be grown at sea level, the better grades are the grades that are grown at higher elevations. Higher elevations slow the growth process, because of the colder air. The slower growth process allows the coffee beans to develop more slowly, which gives them a lot more flavor. The growth can be further slowed by planting the coffee in the shade of existing trees (shade-grown coffee).

Producing shade-grown coffee has the added benefit of encouraging "biodiversity," which means that there are enough different levels in the food chain present to make growing coffee possible without insecticides. The coffee can also be produced without chemical fertilizers. Coffee grown closer to sea level in vast wide open fields has to be fertilized and sprayed with insecticides, and grows too fast to be very good. See Figure 1, which shows a young coffee plant.

Once coffee is picked, it is sorted to remove sticks, leaves, unripe cherries, overripe cherries, and the like. Then, it is processed by either the wet or dry process, to remove the outer hulls. This leaves the inside bean halves, which range in color from tan to a dark blue-green. The color is actually largely influenced by the processing method, with the wet process yielding a blue-green bean and dry process yielding a more yellow or tan bean.

Figure 1

The wet or dry method is selected based primarily on the climate. The beans can't be properly dried in a humid or rainy climate, and the wet process can't be properly used in a dry or desert-like climate with limited water availability. The process converts the coffee cherries into the green beans that eventually wind up at roasters. The wet process entails using a water bath to separate and clean the coffee. After the coffee is separated, it is dried to reduce water content to 10-12%. The dry process forgoes the wet bath and simply involves drying the beans until the husks can be easily separated.

Once the green coffee has been processed, it is graded (classified) for defects and "cupped" (sampled) for flavor, and bagged and exported. The importer cups the coffee before buying it, and when it is received, has it available for the roaster to sample before the roaster buys it. Usually, roasters have well established relationships with their importers, which allow them to forego the process of cupping the coffee themselves, in favor of relying on the judgment of the importer. (Learning to cup coffee takes time to develop the sampler's palate, and is not practical for making purchasing decisions for new cuppers for several months.)

Once the roaster receives the coffee, it is generally test-roasted to determine the optimum roast. Interestingly, coffees from different areas in the same country will frequently do best with entirely different roasts. The coffee is roasted to bring out the best flavor for that particular bean. Some coffees take to a "high" or dark roast very well, but with some coffees, a dark roast will mask all the interesting characteristics of the coffee. As a general rule, the denser or harder the bean, the longer the roast.

There are actually several different roasting methods that impart different flavors to the coffee. Coffee can be slow roasted in micro roasters that vary in capacity from a few pounds to 25 pounds (see Figure 2), or they can be roasted in huge commercial roasters that roast upwards of 600 pounds at a time. The smaller roasters tend to roast at lower temperatures for longer times. 10-12 minutes at 425-500 degrees would be typical. The larger commercial roasters are more interested in cranking out the coffee as quickly as possible, and can actually roast off 1500 pounds of coffee in as little as 90 seconds by using extremely high temperatures. (See Figures 3 and 4)

In the smaller roasters, the coffee can be fire-roasted or air-bed roasted. The smaller roasters are usually computer controlled, although a few antique roasters still are used where the coffee is roasted by hand and its doneness determined by smell and visual clues. (Figure 4b) The roasters that use these hand roasters are generally more knowledgeable in their coffees than the roasters that rely strictly on computer controls.

After roasting, the coffee is then ground according to the intended method of brewing. Espresso methods take a fine grind, for example, and French Presses take a very coarse grind. The different grinds are essential to producing the best possible coffee according to the selected preparation technique.

If fine ground coffee is used with a French Press, the coffee will pass though the screen and wind up in your cup, and if a coarse grind is used in espresso, the water passes through the coffee too quickly, and the result is a weak and bitter espresso.

Figure 2

Figure 3

The finest grind is called a Turkish Grind, and is used in the Turkish method of preparing coffee by boiling the grounds. (Contrary to popular belief, coffee does not actually grow in Turkey; Turkish coffee refers to the grind and the method of preparation.) As the coffee becomes more and more coarse, the preparation methods traverse the scale from Turkish to Espresso to Drip to Percolate to French Press.

Figure 4

Figure 4b

After preparation, the coffee can be had straight by the cup, turned into one of those great lattes, or enjoyed simply as a strong shot of espresso or as an Americano. In fact, espresso can be made every bit as good with a home espresso machine as it can be made from a $7,000.00 espresso machine! (See Chapter 6 for exact instructions and trade secrets for making that perfect espresso at home.)

So, with good fresh coffee and the proper preparation technique, perfect coffee can be had every time!

# Chapter Three How Coffee is Graded

L ike most agricultural products, coffee is graded. The higher the grade, the more premium the coffee, and the higher the price per pound. Coffee grades are generally established by the country of origin, and there is sometimes not much consistency in the grading classifications. But, as with other agricultural products, the taste is the ultimate determination!

## *Grades*

Coffee is graded according to the size of the bean, and the number of defects in the sample. The size of the bean ranges from Small to Very Large (very original!) as follows:

Small

Medium

Large

Very Large

In Colombian coffees, the smaller beans are graded Excelso, and the larger beans are graded Supremo. In the African and Indian grading systems, the largest beans are AAA as in Zimbabwe AAA, and then the grades run downward in decreasing size to AA, A, B, and C, and then the small round beans are Peaberries.

The size is determined by screen, in which coffees are "sifted" through screens of decreasing hole size to sort them. The screens are numbered from 14 to 20, the number being the numerator in a fraction whose denominator is always 64. Thus, we have as the most common screen sizes:

| Screen | Bean Size |
|--------|-----------|
| 20 | 20/64" |
| 18 | 18/64" |
| 16 | 16/64" |
| 14 | 14/64" |

Interestingly enough, although one would assume that the 20/64" is the largest dimension (or length) of the bean, it's actually the shortest dimension of the bean. I didn't figure this out for myself until I actually made a screen out of paper to verify screen size and couldn't figure out why all the beans seemed the wrong size! You can make representations of the different screen sizes. If you are adventurous, you can cut them out and feed beans through them! See Figure 5 for an idea of the different sized beans. The figure shows smaller beans on the left, larger beans on the right, and a small and a large next to each other for comparison.

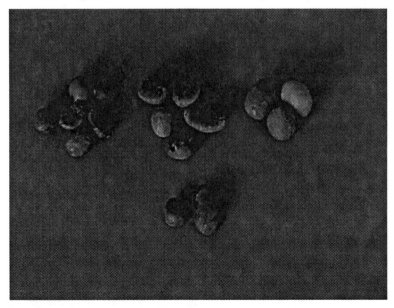

Figure 5

Another consideration in grading coffee is the number of defects. Being an agricultural product, there will be a certain number of beans that didn't grow right and are misshapen, or that were picked while still too green (and don't roast up right), and there will be a certain inclusion of sticks, husks, stones, bark, and other foreign objects. Naturally, these all throw the flavor off, so it's desirable to have as few defects as possible. The coffee is graded by obtaining a small sample of 300g, and basically identifying and counting the defects.

The major defects are as follows:

Primary Defects:

> Full Black
> Full Sour
> Dried Cherry Pod
> Fungus Damaged
> Severe Insect Damage
> Foreign Matter

Secondary Defects:

> Partial Black
> Partial Sour
> Parchment
> Floater
> Immature/Unripe
> Shell
> Broken/Chipped/cut
> Hull/Husk
> Slight Insect Damage

The defects are named for the type of defect, and are generally pretty self-explanatory. Black beans are beans that died or were overly ripe and are shriveled and black. Fungus damage can occur during the growth of the cherry, and floaters are less dense beans that were not fully ripe. Insect damage can range from a pinhole in the side of the bean to the majority of the bean being missing. Hulls and husks are chips of the outside of the bean that make it through processing, and broken/chipped/cut beans were damaged somewhere along the line. Coffee is generally machine sorted to remove as many defects as possible, but many countries actually hand-sort the processed green beans because of the inexpensive labor supply.

Once the coffee is graded, it is categorized according to the number and type (primary or secondary) of defects that were found. See figure 6 for some defects. Broken beans are shown on the left, insect damage is shown in the top bean, and partial black beans are shown on the right.

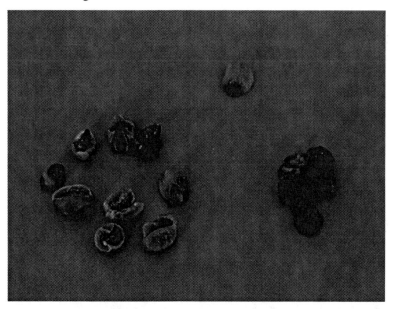

Figure 6

In other words, Specialty Grade coffee can have none of the most serious "Primary" defects, and only 5 of the less serious "Secondary" defects per 300g sample. As the grade decreases, the number and type of allowable defects increases.

The major grading categories are as follows:

| Grade | Defects Allowed | |
| --- | --- | --- |
| | Primary | Secondary |
| Specialty Grade | None | 5 |
| Premium Grade | OK | 8 |
| Exchange Grade | OK | 9-23 |
| Below Standard Grade | OK | 24-86 |
| Off Grade | OK | >86 |

Specialty grade coffee will have the fewest defects and the most perfect beans, and will result in the best cup. Remember, the lower the grade, the more defects. Figure 7 shows specialty grade coffee. Note the single defect, slight insect damage, on the bean in the upper left corner.

Figure 7

As strange as it may seem, there's a movement afoot right now that generally reads that if coffee is less than half real coffee, which is what most grocery store canned coffee is, that it must be labeled "coffee byproducts" instead of coffee. Who knows if that'll fly! Big coffee companies aren't in a big hurry to identify that their coffee is less than 50% coffee, but on the other hand, if a company is doing 100% Specialty Grade, 100% Arabica coffee, they probably will make a big deal of it.

Anyway, coffee being a commodity, there is a very strong relationship between price and quality. And, like fine wines, the more it costs, the better it usually is. If it's inexpensive, there's generally a reason why. If the coffee has almost 50% defects, it's just not going to be as good as perfect coffee.

Not to get too technical, but there are grades of defects, as well. In other words, some defects are more tolerable than others. Defects are generally categorized as to how much they throw off the flavor of the coffee. While a slight amount of insect damage is tolerable, for example, severe insect damage is not. Severe insect damage is a Category 1 (primary) defect, not allowed in Specialty Grade coffee. Slight insect damage, a Category 2 (secondary) Defect, is allowable in Premium Grade coffee. In the lower grades, the bean can be half gone from insect damage. This obviously throws off the taste much more than a bean with a little nibble out of it! The rough edge from insect damage burns during roasting, causing bitterness.

And, last but not least, comes ungraded coffee. Basically, ungraded coffee includes the full range of beans and defects, and includes the good, the bad, and the ugly. This is what results if one buys all the coffee that comes off an estate in a year's crop. So, when those big coffee chains brag about buying a plantation's entire crop, what they are getting is ungraded coffee.

## *Certifications*

Upper-end coffees are generally certified as one or more of several certifications, and once certified, are packaged in bags that also bear the certification. (Figure 8 shows the bag of a certified organic, certified Fair Trade coffee from Peru.)

Figure 8

## Coffee

We've put this here because of legislation called "The Coffee Purity Act of 2002" working its way through Congress. This Act would define coffee entering the USA as containing no more than 86 defects per 350 g sample for Arabica beans, and no more than 150 defects per 375 g sample for Robusta beans. Coffee that did not meet this standard would have to be labeled as "Coffee By-product." This legislation is (needless to say) getting quite a fight from large coffee importers who shall remain nameless but we all know who they are. Anyway, it's anyone's guess whether this legislation will pass, but apparently it's an effort to conform to already existing Resolution 407, of the International Coffee Organization (ICO).

# Fair Trade

Fair Trade Coffee is certified by Transfair USA, an independent certifying organization. Transfair USA ensures that the farmers receive a fair price for their coffee, and they monitor the coffee from the farmer to the exporter to the importer to the roaster. Coffee that is Fair Trade Certified has met the criteria that the farmer receives a minimum price, which is generally well in excess of the market price for coffee. This ensures a higher standard of living for the farmers, who often live in poverty in third world countries. Becoming certified by Transfair USA is a long process of verifications and monitoring, to ensure that only Fair Trade coffee is labeled as such. Use of the Fair Trade logo requires licensing by the roaster and payment of royalties. Coffees that are Fair Trade Certified bear the following logo:

# Shade Grown

Shade grown coffee is coffee grown under the shade of other trees. Large coffee plantations generally plant & harvest in the equivalent manner as strip-mining. All indigenous vegetation is cleared away for the planting of coffee crops. Conversely, in shade grown coffee, the coffee plants are grown in the shade of existing vegetation.

This is better for biodiversity, which is one of the things that allows for organically grown coffee. With a biodiverse environment, there is less need for chemical pesticides and fertilizers.

Additionally, the coffee tastes better, because the plants mature slower, the beans grow slower, and develop a more rich taste. Quickly grown coffee has kind of a flat taste.

## Organic

Organic coffees come in two varieties: passive organic and certified organic. Passive organic means that the coffee has been grown without the use of chemicals or pesticides, but you have to take the farmers' word for it. Certified Organic coffee has been certified by one of the internationally recognized certifying organizations, like the Organic Crop Improvement Association. Certified Organic coffee bears the following logo:

The rules for Organic Certification changed in September of 2002, and are now more uniform. For a farm to become certified takes 3 years of monitoring and soil sample testing, a long and tedious process. Additionally, with the new regulations, coffee roasters are required to be certified to identify their coffee as organic. This generally involved having separate equipment for processing and handling the organic coffee, so it is not contaminated by non-organic coffee.

## Bird Friendly

Bird Friendly Coffee is certified as such by the Smithsonian Migratory Bird Center in Washington. Although similar to shade grown coffee, bird friendly coffee has additional criteria. "Bird

Friendly®" coffees are shade-grown and organic. The alternative way of growing coffee entails cutting down the canopy trees and growing coffee plants under full sun. These "sun coffee" farms provide little or no bird habitat and pollute the environment because they require large amounts of chemical pesticides and fertilizers.

The following material was reprinted from the Smithsonian National Zoological Park website:

**How do "Bird Friendly®" coffees taste compared to other coffees?** Coffee experts say that shade-grown coffees taste better than sun-grown coffees. This is because shade coffee beans ripen more slowly, resulting in a richer flavor. However, because of recent changes in coffee production and marketing, shade coffee plantations are a threatened habitat. In the past twenty years, coffee has begun to be grown with no shade canopy at all. While this manner of cultivation produces substantially increased yields, these cannot be sustained for many years without intensive management (additions of chemical fertilizers and a range of insecticides, herbicides and fungicides); they are also subject to premature death in environments possessing a marked dry season, and they need to be renovated (plants replaced) much more frequently than the shade varieties. sun coffee production has resulted in major habitat change for migratory birds in the past two decades. Of the permanent cropland planted in coffee, the amount under modern, reduced-shade coffee systems ranges from 17% in Mexico to 40% in Costa Rica and 69% in Colombia. The few studies that have been conducted have found that the diversity of migratory birds plummets when coffee is converted from shade to sun. One study found a decrease from 10 to 4 common species of migratory birds. As for the overall avifauna, studies in Colombia and Mexico found 94-97% fewer bird species in sun grown coffee than in shade grown coffee. This comes as no surprise since over two-thirds of the birds are found in the canopy of shade plantations and less than 10% are found foraging in coffee plants. Shade trees protect the understory coffee plants from rain and sun, help maintain soil quality, reduce the need for weeding, and aid in pest control. Organic matter from the shade trees also provides a natural mulch, which reduces the need for chemical fertilizers, reduces erosion, contributes important nutrients to the soil, and prevents metal toxicities.

For the entire text, visit:
http://nationalzoo.si.edu/ConservationAndScience/MigratoryBirds/ Fact_Sheets/default.cfm?fxsht=1

## Rainforest Alliance

The Rainforest Alliance is a relative newcomer to the coffee scene, and was formed in 1987. Their objective is similar to that of the Smithsonian's Bird Friendly program, to promote biodiversity and sustainable farming practices. As of this writing, they had 25,000 members and supporters, an annual budget of 8.8 million, and 81 employees. The Alliance licenses companies to use their logo on their products if the goals of the Alliance are met in the production of the product. The Alliance has only recently become affiliated with coffee, and historically has pursued other avenues to achieve their objectives. We expect to see more and more of the Alliance as people become more and more familiar with their work.

# Chapter Four How to Store Coffee

The natural enemies of coffee are heat, light, and oxygen. Therefore, proper storage of coffee means keeping it cool, dry, and away from oxygen. Kind of like mushrooms, but not quite!

Although coffee can easily be kept cool and dark, keeping it away from oxygen is a little trickier. As soon as coffee is roasted, the oxygenation process starts, and the coffee begins to lose freshness. About the only way to minimize this effect is to drink the coffee as soon after roasting as possible.

No matter how good the coffee starts out, by the time it's a few months old, it's going to be stale. Freezing slows this process somewhat, but unfortunately it also introduces other problems like freezer-burn, and the undesirable congealing of oils on the surface of darker roasted beans. Purists who can't buy coffee every few days have been known to vacuum pack their coffee, in those little home food sealing units. This slows the degeneration considerably, although nothing stops it altogether.

Putting coffee in the refrigerator doesn't do much to preserve it either, although many people swear by it. If it's not perfectly sealed, it can pick up refrigerator odors, not unlike a box of baking soda. So, your best bet is to keep it in an airtight container in the cupboard.

One thing that will help to preserve coffee is to buy it whole bean and grind it as you need it. Ground coffee has greatly increased surface area, which will cause it to go stale much quicker. Because it's the surface of the coffee that mixes with oxygen to get stale, minimizing the surface area slows the process. So, with whole bean coffee, the beans are still fresh on the inside even as the outside begins to stale.

The other important thing to consider is how old the coffee is when you buy it. Many coffee companies are now dating their coffee, either with the date spelled out in months and days, or by coding it into their product codes. The coffee can be dated in one of two ways, so caution is needed in determining what the date on the bag is telling you. The date can either be the roast date, in which case the date would obviously be earlier than the purchase date, or it could be the expiration date, which hopefully is a future date. So, just because the date on the bag has passed, doesn't mean you are buying old coffee.

Another thing to watch with the dates is how far in the future the expiration dates go. This can usually be accomplished by checking several bags. Some will have an expiration date within a few weeks, and some will go out several months. This information can be used to determine what produce shelf life is assigned to the coffee, and can help you determine its freshness. For example, if you see two bags on a shelf and one has a few weeks left and the other has six months left, the first one has obviously been sitting on the shelf for almost six months, so even though it is technically still within date, it is actually almost six months old. It would be better to buy the bag with the more distant expiration date, even if it's not your first choice in variety, because the coffee will be fresher and better.

Decaffeinated coffees are even more critical as far as buying fresh. Because of the somewhat aggressive decaffeination process, decaffeinated coffee goes stale much faster than regular coffee. Coffee is decaffeinated by either a chemical process or a natural water process. Chemically decaffeinated coffee uses chemicals to strip the caffeine, and water bath decafs are soaked in water, which forces out the caffeine, as well as much of the flavor. The water is then filtered to remove the caffeine, and then the beans are re-soaked in the coffee flavored water to return the coffee flavor to the beans. This temporary separation of the flavor from the beans results in a shorter lifespan for the coffee.

Flavored coffee is another coffee where freshness is critical. In addition to the coffee going stale, the flavoring syrups can go stale. The flavoring syrups can actually be stale before they are even put on the coffee. Most small roasters are unaware of this fact, and keep an inventory of flavoring syrups on the shelf for months and years, when actually the flavoring syrups have a one year shelf life, whether or not they have been opened. After the one year, the flavoring syrups have almost totally dissipated, and if the roaster continues to use them, what you buy will be sticky coffee with no flavor at all. But, even if the syrups are only a few months old when the roaster uses them, if the coffee you buy is six months old, that puts the syrups pretty much at the end of their lifespan, and in addition to getting coffee that is stale, the flavoring is stale, resulting in a disappointing cup.

One way to know for sure that you've gotten stale coffee is to take it home, open it, be greeted with that nice coffee aroma, but the next day there is no aroma at all. What you got when you first opened it was that last little breath of life the coffee had, and now you're left with a full container of coffee way past its lifespan.

Larger commercial coffee producers will flush their coffee with nitrogen to remove oxygen and attempt to extend the lifespan. This will extend the shelf life somewhat, but once the coffee is opened, the aging process proceeds with a vengeance.

And, not to make things too complicated, coffee that is fresh out of the roaster will have almost no aroma at all. This is because once the coffee has been roasted, it "degasses" in 2-5 days, which is when the aroma is at its height. So, if you purchase coffee directly from a roaster who says the coffee was roasted that very day, don't expect to open it at home and be greeted with a rush of aromas. Instead, wait until the next day, and you will get a pleasant surprise!

# Chapter Five How to Make Coffee

No coffee book would really be complete without a few
words on how to make coffee and the principles involved.
The idea of brewing coffee is to get out as much of the
good stuff as you can while leaving all the stuff that makes the
coffee bitter. The best coffee in the world can yield a bitter cup if
it's not prepared properly. The different compounds that produce
bitter flavors and desirable flavors come out of the ground coffee
at different temperatures and pressures. Each method of brewing
coffee gets different compounds; some get more of the good, some
get more of the bad, and some get more of the downright ugly.

The absolute best way to separate the good from the bad is with
an espresso machine that produces adequate pressure. The best way
to explain the principle is to compare it with a pressure car wash.
If you hose down a car, you get the surface material off, but to get
down deep and get the good stuff, a pressure wand is needed. But, if
the pressure is too high, you'll go right down into the clearcoat and
paint, definitely not a good idea. So, with this process, the oils and
desirable compounds are "washed" off the beans, leaving the bitter
compounds behind.

The pressure is there to increase temperature and speed up the
process so it is completed before the bitterness starts to show up.
The high temperature is very important. Unlike tea, which can be
satisfactorily made by steeping tea leaves in water even at room
temperature (sunshine tea), coffee absolutely needs the higher
temperatures. Imagine what coffee would taste like if the heating

element in the machine were working at half capacity and water of only 140° came through the coffee. You'd wind up with coffee so thin that it would be undrinkable.

There's a time element involved, too. With an espresso machine, it takes approximately 20-30 seconds to get all the good stuff out, and then the bitter stuff follows. Getting this down right is difficult (but not impossible) with a home espresso machine; in fact the overwhelming majority of commercial shops don't get it right either. (See the chapter on "How to make a $7,000.00 cup of espresso with a $70.00 home espresso machine" for details on how to work a home espresso machine. That chapter gives more detail on why home espresso machines often produce bitter coffee—the extraction goes on for too long and after the good stuff is extracted, the bitter stuff comes out into the cup as well.)

If you want just a cup of coffee and not an espresso drink, dilute the shot of espresso with hot water, which yields an Americano. This is the best coffee there is, because the process captures all the essential oils in the coffee, which is where a lot of the flavor is.

The next best way to get a good cup a' joe is to use a French Press. Again, this process keeps the essential oils in the coffee, although the method doesn't extract as much of the oils as the pressure espresso method. With a French Press, the grounds and hot water are mixed and then separated by forcing a screen down through the drink. The screen captures the grounds in the bottom, and the coffee is poured off the top. This is good, because the oils float on the coffee, and with the grounds at the bottom, the oils can be poured off with the coffee. Oils on the top of the coffee are very desirable; without them it is just weak coffee.

Next down the hierarchy is regular brewed coffee. This is third on the list because with the grounds on top and the coffee filtered out the bottom, the oils sit on top of the grounds and are thrown away. The other factor that throws off brewed coffee is the temperature of the water. Did you ever wonder why the same coffee tastes so good in a restaurant but the very same coffee tastes weak and devoid of flavor and body when brewed at home? Commercial coffee makers brew the coffee at higher temperatures. The coffee made with a home coffee machine comes out at a dismal 160°, as opposed to commercial machines, where the water comes out at 185° which makes the difference.

If you really like the convenience of brewing coffee at home with a brewing machine, consider spending $200.00 at a restaurant supply house for a commercial machine. Not only is the coffee better, but it's faster, it will last a lifetime, and they are typically easier to clean. They are faster because they brew coffee on demand, because the water is kept hot inside the holding tank. The only concern is that the water will eventually evaporate off if they are not used often enough, so if you want to invest in a commercial machine for home use, don't let it sit for weeks without using it. Home coffee machines in the higher price ranges are coming out that will brew professional quality coffee; check the internet or upscale stores for availability.

Moving further down the scale comes percolator coffee, which pretty much combines all the bad methods together. There is no way to control the process, because you continue to boil the coffee until it turns a color you like, and boiling the coffee inevitably results in the compounds that cause bitter coffee to wind up in your drink. This is a great method if you are camping out and want that campfire coffee taste, but that's about where its novelty ends.

Also worthy of brief mention is Turkish coffee, a method of preparing coffee that results in about two thirds of a cup of odd coffee with about one third of a cup of sludge in the bottom. It's prepared by boiling coffee that has been pulverized way past espresso grind. Commercial grinders like the ones they let customers use in grocery stores have a Turkish grind setting, all the way to the right of the dial. Try it once as a novelty!

In case you've ever wondered why coffee instructions say to make the coffee with cold water instead of hot, there are two reasons for this. First, the principle is that cold water is fresher and hasn't been sitting in a hot water heater for days, although you have to be pretty fanatical to be able to taste the difference. (Try a blind taste test some lazy Sunday afternoon to see if you can tell the difference!) The second reason is that using hot water will turn off the burner element in some home coffee machines, because the thermostat tells the system the water is hot already. When this happens, the water doesn't really get hot enough, and you wind up with weak coffee.

One of the characteristics of coffee that is lost if the coffee is not made with an espresso machine or French Press is body. The body of coffee is actually created by the oils in the coffee, and if these are thrown away with the grounds, the body, or feeling of fullness in the mouth, is lost. The other characteristics of coffee, such as acidity and fragrance, will survive the other methods, although not in their entirety.

In summary, the best coffee in the world will produce a substandard cup if prepared improperly. An investment in gourmet coffee really demands an investment in the proper brewing equipment.

# Chapter Six What are the Different Kinds of Roasts?

Coffees can be roasted to a varied degree of "doneness." Although they have different names, there are basically five categories of roasts.

1. Light      Light colored with dry surface
2. Regular    familiar brown with dry surface
3. Full       darker brown with a "semi-gloss" finish
4. Italian    darker brown with a shine of oil
5. Heavy      almost black with a definite "gloss"

In a light, or cinnamon roast, the coffee flavors are not fully developed, thus it is common to continue the roasting through this stage. (Unless you are roasting the coffee to "cup" it, in which case you would stop your roast now.)

An American, or regular roast, leaves beans with a rich, sweet flavor, but with none of the bittersweet taste associated with darker roasts.

Continued roasting results in full, light French or light espresso. The bittersweet flavors are beginning to appear at this stage.

Roasting even further results in an Italian or French, in which most traces of acidity are gone.

Roasting to the final stages gives a Dark French or heavy roast. At this point, the coffee has an almost charcoal tone along with the characteristic bitterness; all acidity tones are gone. Figure 9 shows green beans on the left and fully roasted beans on the right.

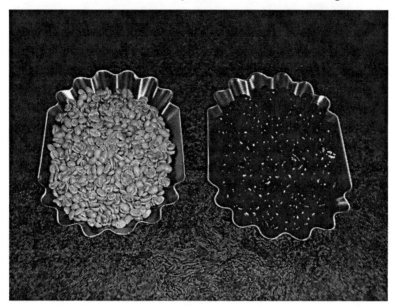

Figure 9

Different beans "take" a different roast, to bring out the best the bean has to offer. Some are best with a lighter roast, and some beans are definitely better with a dark roast. And, it depends on the characteristics the roaster wants to bring out in the bean. For example, a Nicaraguan coffee is generally fairly light and acidic, characteristics that are best brought out by a regular, or medium roast. However, if the exact same bean is roasted to an Italian roast, the lightness and snappiness completely disappears, and is replaced by a much fuller body and stronger flavor. So, if you wanted a coffee for a breakfast blend, Nicaragua would work, but if you wanted to slip a little into your espresso blend, as long as it was roasted longer, it would work fine for that, too. Actually, the best way to summarize it is to compare it to wines, and the age-old topic of whether to drink white or red with fish or meat. The bottom line is this: drink what YOU like!

Unfortunately, there is no standardization in the roast of coffee; it is highly subjective and depends on the name given by the roaster.

And, to further complicate matters, the different roasts each can be known by four or five different names. For example, a medium roast can be known as regular, American, Medium Brown, or Medium High. A dark roast can be known as Italian, Espresso, European, French After dinner, Continental, or dark. And, to make matters worse, one coffee purveyor might refer to a roast as French, and another might think the same roast is only a high roast. Confusing? Yes, but the best way to tell is to try the coffee!

Coffee is roasted in coffee roasters that vary considerably in size. Specialty roasters generally use batch roasters that roast 12-24 pounds at a time. The newer models are computer controlled, and roasters end the roasting cycle when a pre-determined temperature is reached. Older roasting machines have only a "sampler," a small cylinder which removes a small sample of beans for inspection by the roaster. Hand roasting is a preferable method in the hands of an experienced roaster, because the roaster is more in tune with the beans than a computer operator would be.

Larger commercial roasters can roast upwards of 600 pounds at a time, and the process is carefully controlled. Imagine burning 600 pounds of coffee! But, the artisan character is lost when so much is computer-roasted at a time. The large commercial roasters also use a hot air bed instead of a flame, which some believe is akin to baking a steak instead of broiling it.

The smaller specialty roasters work by dumping green coffee beans from a chute into a rotating cylinder or drum, which is heated by gas flames. When the desired degree of roast is achieved, the beans are dumped into a large cooling tray that rapidly cools the beans to halt the roast. The beans are generally cooled to room temperature within five minutes, and can then be packaged. Immediate packaging of the beans slows the staling process considerably by reducing the exposure to oxygen. Beans that are left exposed to the elements in clear acrylic containers stale within days. They are fun to look at, but if fresh coffee is your goal, go for the packaged coffee. (Of course, the other problem with those acrylic containers is that they *never* get washed, and oils on the sides can turn sour and contaminate the beans.)

Anyway, whatever your current preferences in coffee, feel free to experiment with different blends and roasts and most importantly, enjoy!

# Chapter Seven How is Coffee Flavored?

offee is flavored with a special flavoring syrup after it is
roasted. The best flavor results from cooling the coffee first,
although some roasters like to flavor the coffee when it is still
very hot. Flavoring hot coffee allows some of the aromatics of the
flavoring to vaporize, and releases some of the flavor, which is why
coffee should always be flavored after it has cooled. The flavoring
is something that is actually picked up by your nose, not your taste
buds. Taste buds are only capable of distinguishing between sweet,
sour, salty, and bitter. Your nose can distinguish between 2000 and
4000 flavors, depending on how "well trained" it is.

Basically, the different flavors are either added straight to the
coffee, or blended for a unique taste. For example, a butterscotch-
chestnut-vanilla coffee is a combination of butterscotch and chestnut
with a hint of vanilla.

Unfortunately, it is a common practice among roasters to use
stale beans and mask them with flavors; it is important to find a
roaster who uses the freshest Arabica beans for the best in flavor!
Another common practice is to flavor over only inexpensive grades
of beans. We find it better to flavor over more interesting coffee, for
more depth and satisfaction in the final cup.

Interestingly, the flavoring syrups have a shelf life just like the
coffee, so it is important to have fresh flavoring for the coffee as
well. Once flavoring syrups get more than a year old, the flavor
dissipates entirely. So with old flavored coffee, not only are the
beans stale, but the flavoring has faded as well.

Flavoring the coffee beans themselves gives a flavored coffee with no added sugar or calories. The other way to flavor coffee is with those wonderful latte syrups, as described more fully in the chapters on coffee drinks. Unfortunately, they add a few calories to the drinks. But, for a special treat, it's definitely worth it!

# Chapter Eight How is Coffee Decaffeinated?

There are several methods of decaffeination available to processors, but in general it is an expensive process requiring significant investments in plant and equipment. In general, coffee can be chemically decaffeinated or water decaffeinated. Water decaffeination is the preferred method for obvious reasons.

## *Water Process Decaffeination*

Water process decaffeination is where the green coffee beans are soaked in water, which winds up with the caffeine by osmosis and most of the flavor as well. The water is then decaffeinated, and the beans returned to soak in the water to kind of transfer the flavor back over to the beans. In the water process, the water is filtered to remove the caffeine. It's interesting that filtering the water will remove the caffeine but not the flavor, although some flavor will still be lost just by the nature of the process. When the flavor has been re-infused back into the beans, the beans are dried and sent to the roaster. (Roasters never decaffeinate their own beans, just because of the enormous expense of the equipment.)

When the roaster receives the beans, great care must be taken in roasting them. The process changes the roasting characteristics, making the coffee much more sensitive to heat and therefore easier to burn. Also, the "cracking" sounds that are pronounced in roasting caffeinated beans are muted, and much more difficult to hear when roasting decaffeinated beans. This lack of audible progress indicators also makes it much easier to burn decaffeinated beans.

## Chemically Decaffeinated Coffee

Chemically decaffeinated coffee is processed with the use of some scary sounding chemicals, like methelyne chloride and methyl alcohol. The chemicals have all been identified as safe, however, and to be honest, most chemical traces burn off in roasting.

There are some people who think that formaldehyde is used in processing coffee; this is simply not true. Unfortunately, people hear rumors like this and then repeat them, and the rumors gain a life of their own. So, although the process is aggressive to remove the caffeine, no dangerous chemicals are ever used.

## Different Caffeine Levels In Different Species Of Beans

The two main types of coffee beans, Robusta and Arabica, have different caffeine levels. If you are a caffeine junkie, and drink coffee only for the caffeine, Robusta is the way to go. (Think Folgers and Maxwell House.) Robusta actually has a higher caffeine level than Arabica, although if you're drinking coffee for the flavor and the experience, the relatively lower level in Arabica is not really noticeable.

## How the Roast Affects the Caffeine Level

There are many chemical changes that happen when coffee is roasted; a reduction in the amount of caffeine is one of them. For pure caffeine junkies, there is a small cult of drinkers of "white coffee," which is coffee that is barely roasted and remains kind of tan looking. This renders the highest amount of caffeine possible, although words fail us when trying to describe the taste. Much better to get caffeine tablets or maybe caffeine patches! (Some enterprising entrepreneur will eventually bring something like that to market! If you decide to do that, don't forget where you got the idea!)

# Chapter Nine What Makes Gourmet Coffee Gourmet?

The dictionary definition of gourmet is: food involving exotic and high quality ingredients, prepared in a skillful way.

Gourmet coffee differs from grocery store coffee in many ways. First, there are two very different main species of coffee, Arabica and Robusta. Robusta is considerably less expensive and is commonly used in mass distributed coffees. Robusta grows faster with a larger yield, but produces an inferior flavor. Arabica is a premium species of coffee that simply results in a superior flavor. So, the first criterion of gourmet, high quality ingredients, is met with coffee from specialty coffee roasters, since they use only Arabica beans. And, using only Specialty grade coffee further contributes to premium flavor. Remember, coffee is available in five different grades, Specialty being the best grade, followed by Premium, then Standard, and you don't really want to know the other two. (But in case you really do, the other two grades are Exchange and Off-grade. Ever wonder where that coffee winds up? It sure doesn't get thrown out because it's "off grade!")

The region also determines the final flavor of the coffee. Coffee is grown at high altitudes, around the world near the equator. Only Hawaii grows coffee in the United States, the rest of the coffee is from South America, Indonesia, India, Africa, and other exotic places.

Once the coffee is selected, it is roasted to the desired doneness. This can be done in several different ways, from air roasting at 600° for 90 seconds a load (common) to Fire Roasting at lower temperatures for as much as forty five minutes. The difference is the same as the difference between a BBQ'd steak and a baked steak! Remember, there are over 800 distinct molecular compounds in coffee. Preparing one way will bring out chocolate, cinnamon, and flowers. Preparing another way will bring out sulfur, smoke, and rancid flavors. Coffee that is Fire Roasted at low temperatures (425°) for longer periods of time brings out the best essence of the coffee.

Most coffees today are computer roasted, and the computer tells the operator when the coffee is "done." We believe that hand roasting coffee and determining "doneness" by smell, color, oil production, and texture produces a superior product that can truly be called Gourmet Coffee!

Flavored coffees come in different grades, as well, with flavoring syrups ranging considerably in price as well as quality. The better gourmet coffees have been flavored with the better syrups, syrups that are made with natural ingredients instead of artificial ingredients.

Decaffeinated coffees have a huge range in quality as well. Coffees can be chemically decaffeinated or decaffeinated with the water process; both yield different flavor profiles. The quality and grade of the coffee that is decaffeinated also affects the final product. A better grade of coffee bean will yield a better grade of decaffeinated coffee.

Last, but not least, the best gourmet product in the world will be no better than average unless it is brought to you fresh! Ever notice how many gourmet coffees lose that great aroma the day after they're opened? Find a source for coffee that roasts fresh and provides fresh coffee, and develop a relationship with them, and then you can be sure of getting what you're paying for!

# Chapter Ten What are Estate Coffees?

The easiest way to explain what estate coffees are is to compare them to estate wines. People are familiar with what allows estate wines to command prices that are several multiples of the prices commanded by blended wines. As it turns out, coffee beans are similar to wine grapes in many ways. Wine connoisseurs with developed palates can identify different wines from different estates just by tasting the wine. When an estate produces an exceptional wine, it commands an exceptional price that connoisseurs are willing to pay because they know they will have a sought-after and rare quality wine.

Just like wine connoisseurs have their favorite estates for wine, coffee connoisseurs have their favorite estates for coffee. And, just like wine connoisseurs have their favorite regions for wine (think Napa, Bordeaux, Burgundy regions), coffee connoisseurs have their favorite regions for coffee. Ethiopia, for example, produces coffees from at least 3 distinct regions, Sidamo, Harrar, and Yirgacheffe, each having a distinguishable taste. Closer to home, Guatamala has several coffee producing regions, each with their own flavor characteristics, the most popular being Antigua.

Going one step further, like wine connoisseurs have their own favorite countries for wine, like France, Germany, Italy, United States (California), coffee connoisseurs have their favorite countries, too. Some prefer the softness of Kenya and Hawaiin coffees, some prefer the spicy earthy taste of Ethiopians and Indonesians, some prefer the relative sweetness of Colombian coffees, and some prefer the bold full body of Uganda coffee.

Usually, coffee is combined and blended from many different local plantations and sold through co-ops. This causes some of the individual coffee nuances to be lost. The same is true of wine, where table wines produce a kind of flat wine with no real notable distinguishing characteristics. Estate wines, on the other hand, are easily identified for the superior flavor they produce.

Besides the quality variations inherent in any agricultural product, there are quality variations produced by the cultivation of the product. Estate coffee plantations, just like estate vineyards, will tend their plants with more detail and individual attention that mass-produced coffees that will ultimately be blended. The soil and microclimate of an individual estate will also impact the final cup of coffee. Individual estates also tend towards shade-grown coffee, which many feel is superior to sun-grown coffee. They also tend towards organic coffees.

In general, they are less concerned with mass production and more concerned with ensuring that every aspect of the coffee production is of the absolute highest quality, down to the artwork on the bags that carry their products to market. See figure 10, which shows a bag from Doka Estate in Costa Rica. What a work of art!

There are literally hundreds of thousands of coffee producing plantations around the world. Ethiopia alone has over 100,000 coffee producing farms, many only a half acre in size. Once, we were fortunate enough to be able to get some Fair Trade certified coffee from Alto Incariado, a small town in Peru with a population of only 80. What a fun coffee it was!

Figure 10

# Chapter Eleven How to Make a $7,000 Cup of Espresso with a $70 Home Espresso Machine.

This is really the most important chapter in this book. Here, we reveal the secrets on how to make espresso and latte drinks at home that are every bit as good as the espresso and drinks you get at the finest coffee shops, where coffee drinks are made with espresso extracted using the finest $7000.00 espresso machines. (In fact, they could easily be better, because studies have shown that over 90% of espresso machine operators, who work mostly for minimum wage, are making espresso incorrectly.) If you start with a thin, watery, inferior shot of espresso, it just can't be disguised as a good coffee drink, no matter how much milk or flavoring or chocolate or whipped cream you put on it.

Interestingly enough, a home espresso machine will make espresso (almost) every bit as good as the espresso you get in a coffee shop, and the home espresso machine can be had for as little as $70.00. (Figure 11 shows a $70.00 home espresso machine.) In fact, the most important things in making good espresso are really independent of the espresso machine!

By the way, the first thing you want to do when you get this home is to take off the silly little doohickey attached to the steam wand and throw it away. (Figure 12) I have no idea what it's supposed to do, and it's hard to keep it clean.

Figure 11

The next thing is to have fresh high quality coffee, of course. But the most important thing is the grind of the coffee. If it is too coarse, the water will just filter through it like drip coffee, and you'll wind up with thin espresso. (Figure 13 shows perfect espresso on the right, and improperly made espresso on the left.) But, if the grind is too fine, the high-pressure water/steam will find the path of least resistance and make a straight path down to the bottom, which will, ironically, also yield a thin watery espresso. But, if you manage to get the grind just exactly right, the water/steam will come through just right, yielding an excellent cup of espresso with perfect crema on top. The espresso on the left of Figure 13 shows an improperly produced shot of espresso, note the lack of crema, and the right shot shows perfect espresso, with a layer of frothy crema on top.

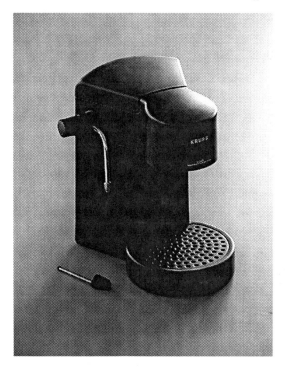

Figure 12

Figure 13

The only way to grind coffee properly is with a burr grinder. A blade grinder yields coffee that is irregular in shape, which will diminish an espresso drink, although it's fine for drip coffee. Another problem with a blade grinder is that the extra time that is required to obtain an espresso type grind is frequently enough to burn the coffee, which will result in a burned taste that can not be covered up or fixed. So, unless you have a burr grinder, and home burr-type grinders are available, your best bet is to get your espresso ground for you when you buy it, using a commercial burr grinder.

A word about "espresso" coffee.... espresso is a method for making coffee, in which super heated pressurized water is forced through coffee grounds to create a thick drink that hopefully has some crema on the top. Espresso is not a type of bean! Usually when a coffee is labeled "espresso" it is a special blend of beans that yield a perfect espresso, and espresso can also be used to describe a roast that is on the darker side, without being excessively oily. Excessive oil will kill the crema, leaving only a flat cup of strong coffee. But, back to how to make perfect espresso.

The next critical step in preparing your coffee for extraction is the tamping. Tamping refers to manually compressing the coffee in the porta-filter, or coffee grounds holding cup. See figure 14 which shows the porta-filter.) Tamping can be accomplished with a tamper that comes with the machine, or you can use the flat base of a wine glass or flat base of a custard cup (being careful not to break it!) or even the flat surface of a bottle of hot sauce (figure 15). The most important thing in tamping coffee is to apply the correct pressure, which is 30 pounds. How do you know when you've applied 30 pounds? Easy! You calibrate your arm with a bathroom scale! Put a scale on the counter at the same height as your tamping operation, and press down until the scale reads 30 pounds. Do this a few times until you remember the pressure, and then tamp down your coffee with the same pressure. Viola! 30 pounds of pressure! Incorrect pressure, incidentally, will yield the same poor results as an incorrect grind.

Figure 14

Figure 15

Once the coffee has been properly tamped (be sure to tamp on a hard surface like a cutting board, to protect your counters), it's time to make the espresso. Assemble the espresso machine according to its directions, and make sure you have TWO containers to catch the coffee. Forget the little glass pitcher that comes with it; it takes too much time to get it out from under the machine when it is time to switch containers. (See figure 16)

Figure 16

Now for the **absolute most important part**! Start the espresso machine, and wait until the coffee starts coming out, hopefully in a thin "rat tail." (If it doesn't come out in a thin rat tail, either the grind or the tamp is wrong.) After about 15 seconds, the crema will begin to appear. After about 15-30 more seconds, the pitch (sound) will begin to change, and the machine will start to put out large bubbles instead of the fine stream, and the crema will start to come out white. (See figure 17, which shows the look of the espresso on the left when it is removed at the proper time, and on the right is espresso that was extracted too long. Notice the presence of large bubbles and white color on the right hand sample.) IMMEDIATELY remove the espresso, and quickly slide in the other container to catch the balance of what comes out. (See figure 18) It is most important to remove your good espresso before the machine starts sputtering and putting out white foam. After the first or second time, you will immediately detect the change and be able to remove your espresso, being sure to replace your container with another, as the machine will put out almost as much volume after you've switched the containers!

Figure 17

Figure 18

Wait until the machine stops, and you will have two completely different products in your two different containers. For amusement's sake, try them both. The first will be an excellent espresso, equal in quality to anything you've ever paid four bucks for. The second will be watery and bitter, and have no useful purpose at all. The reason you wind up with this second cup is that there is too much water for the amount of espresso. Also, after the first 30-45 seconds, all the good stuff is out of the coffee, and as the steam continues to strip the coffee, you wind up with bitterness, thinness, and absolutely no crema. So, in case you had given up on decent home espresso because of previous dismal failures, the problem was in having the two different coffees combined into one, which meant you had all the bitterness and thinness ruining your excellent espresso! One last thing…

When the espresso is done and the milk is frothed, there might still be some water left in the well. Don't turn the machine off until all this water has steamed off! If you do, the water can remain in the espresso machine, past the heater, and will force through your coffee the next time you make espresso. Yuck. Nothing like old cold water messing up your next espresso!

And, don't forget to let some steam run through the steaming wand to clean the inside before the steam is all gone. Interestingly, the steam will heat milk when the wand is in milk, but when you're just blowing off your steam (coffee humor), the steam is cold by the time it's five or six inches away from the wand. For the engineers and scientists out there, that's because $PV=nRT$, but for the rest of us, it just is.

When you are done, and the machine has cooled, you can clean out the porta-filter and confirm your work. The grounds should come out in a solid mass, like a hockey puck. Figure 18 shows the espresso grounds from 3 perfectly extracted shots. Figure 19 shows the grounds that result when the coffee is not ground and tamped properly.

A quick word on frothing milk: there are several different sized pitchers to select from. Figure 20 shows different styles and sizes. The tall one on the upper left is not suitable because the steaming wand will not extend all the way down into the milk. The smaller ones are also not good, because they hold too little milk. Remember, the milk will double in volume if done correctly! Pick the one in the middle, which will hold the milk as it swirls and foams, and will allow you to work your way down into the milk with the wand, thus heating all the milk.

Figure 18

Figure 19

Figure 20

So, now that you've made your first totally perfect espresso, you can be smug in your knowledge that you can have espresso any time you want, and only have to pay four bucks for it at an outside coffee shop if you want to, not because you have to!

After you have made your first shot of perfect espresso, and know what it should really taste like, your coffee expectations will change forever. When you see espresso improperly extracted in coffee shops, you will know why the drink doesn't really have much coffee flavor and instead tastes kind of like sweet hot milk.

These are some of the common mistakes made in commercial espresso stands. First, the espresso shot should take 25-30 seconds to finish extracting. It is interesting to time the shot from when the espresso machine starts to when it finishes. If it takes less than 25 seconds, the espresso will be just like the espresso you made in the second cup in your home coffee making adventure. I personally have seen coffee drink makers use shots in their coffee drinks that have taken less than 10 seconds to make.

In Italy, where they take their espresso seriously enough to drink it straight, espresso machine operators are called Baristas. Baristas spend months learning their trade, and are professionals.

As an example, a true barista will adjust the grind in the grinder throughout the day to compensate for moisture differences in the air, which affect the grind and the extraction. (In constant humidity environments, this isn't as critical as it is on coastal areas, but it is still something to be aware of.) Espresso machine operators in the United States like to call themselves Baristas, but unfortunately most of them do not have the knowledge necessary for this lofty title. In fairness, some do, but most do not.

When you are out buying your first espresso machine, you need to consider how often you will use it and how many drinks you will make at one time. The only real disadvantage to the smaller machines is their "recovery" time, which is how long you have to wait after making an espresso before making the next one. If you have a lot of guests that you want to make espresso drinks for, you will need a bigger machine than the $70.00 ones we've used as examples here. Some of the bigger machines will grind your beans for you as well as making the espresso, and some machines have regular coffee brewers built in. But, if you are just making the drinks for yourself, and just have one or two a day, the little $70.00 machines are more than adequate.

# Chapter Twelve How to Cup Coffee

In this simple and fun procedure, you can easily compare a sample of two or three of your coffees, as well as doing a comparison of your new coffee to your old coffee. It is most important to measure both the coffee and the water carefully, so you are comparing "apples to apples" not "apples to oranges."

You will need a measuring cup for hot water, a teaspoon measurer, a soup spoon, a glass of clean cool water, and enough cups of the same size for each sample. Be careful if using untempered glass or it can break when you add the hot water. Short, wide cups work best. Double shot glasses are available in restaurant supply stores and are the perfect size, although occasionally they will crack from the heat.

First, put one heaping tablespoon of coarsely ground coffee in each cup. Be sure to label the cups! Then, add enough very hot (190°) water to each to cover all the coffee grounds, and bring the level flush to the top of the glass. (Boil the water, then let it sit for a minute or so to cool down to 190.) The coffee will develop a foamy layer on top. Wait 3-4 minutes, then "break" the cup, meaning split the foam with a spoon, being careful not to agitate the foam. (See figure 21, which shows the foam being "broken" and also shows how to set up cupping where you can look at the green beans for defects while sampling the coffee.) Be sure not to stir the coffee! If you stir the coffee, the grounds will settle out of the foam into the coffee, and you'll wind up drinking coffee grounds, a most unpleasant experience! The cupper then immediately "noses" the brew to experience its aroma, an integral step in the evaluation of the coffee's quality.

Figure 21

Wait a few more minutes, and skim the grounds off the top and throw them away. Now for the fun part! Take a spoonful of the coffee from the top, and slurp the coffee from the spoon, making as much noise as you can! That's the easiest way to describe the technique. The objective is to aerate the coffee, so you get the full flavor characteristics. Professional tasters then spit the coffee out, but that's up to you! (Of course, you probably won't be tasting 50-60 cups in one day!)

As you gain experience in cupping coffee, you will begin to notice more subtle differences, but at the beginning you should be able to notice differences in body and acidity. Body is a word describing the "fullness" of the coffee. The richest tasting coffee has the fullest body. One of the coffees should have more body, or fullness, than the others. (It's best to "cup" at least 3 different coffees at the same time, so differences are more easily distinguished.)

Acidity is another characteristic to look for. Acidity is hard to describe, but the best way to describe it is "effervescence." A high acidity coffee will taste like sparkling water, for comparison's sake, and a low acidity coffee will taste like flat water. In coffee, acidity is a prized quality, and has nothing to do with stomach acid or stomach upset.

The more coffees you can sample at one time, the better, as it will allow you to experience a larger range of flavors and aromas. It also allows you to develop reference points in your tastings. If you just sample one coffee, first of all it is a lot of setup for just one sample, but secondly, you can't really tell if it is a full bodied coffee or a weak bodied coffee when you don't have anything to compare it with. If you have 3-5 coffees, you can decide which has the most body and which has the least, and then sort them by amount of body ranging from less to more. Then, when you taste the lower and the higher, you will better understand what is full bodied and what is light bodied.

Light bodied coffee, by the way, is not necessarily undesirable, but instead depends on your personal preferences. Hawaiian Kona is a premium coffee that generally commands $25-30 per pound, and has relatively light body. Most of the African coffees and Indonesian coffees are full bodied. But not all, Zimbabwe and Kenya both tend to produce lighter bodied coffees.

At a roaster or importer, samples from a variety of batches and different beans are tasted. Coffees are not only analyzed this way for their inherent characteristics and flaws, but also for the purpose of blending different beans or determining the proper roast. An expert cupper can taste hundreds of samples of coffee a day and still taste the subtle differences between them. When coffee is professionally cupped, the samples are only roasted to a very light cinnamon roast, which makes the coffee reveal more characteristics for comparison, but also makes it somewhat unsuitable for drinking. So, although you'll need to cup coffee that has been roasted to its best flavor characteristics for drinking (unless you buy it green and roast it yourself in a home roaster), you'll still be able to taste the subtle differences and learn from the cupping experience.

At the end of the book, we have enclosed a sample coffee cupping worksheet, which you can make copies of and use in your cupping. As you perform more cuppings, you will become more familiar with the different tastes and aromas, and be more able to distinguish a high acidity coffee from a low acidity coffee, for example. One thing we've found helpful is to have a standard coffee, a Colombian, for example, as one of the samples each time. That way, you are always comparing your coffee to a standard, which will help you in defining and comparing the coffees. As you become more experienced, and your tongue becomes "calibrated," you won't need the reference coffee anymore.

Enjoy! And remember to keep notes using the worksheet. Not only will this remind you of which taste goes with which coffee, it will help you to remember which is your favorite!

# Chapter Thirteen A Latte by any Other Name...

Figure 22

Looking for something different to do with those lattes? Try some of these delicious recipes! Most require flavored syrups which can be purchased at your local coffee store, or (naturally!) are available on the internet. We recommend Monin syrups, which are premium French syrups, available on the internet.

If you're in a hurry, though, larger cities sell coffee flavoring syrups at local wholesale type stores.

Once you've gotten your syrups and made your perfect espresso, you are ready to turn your drink into something special! And, now that you've completed chapter 8, and know how to make a perfect shot of espresso, you can make these great drinks at home! And, to make them extra special, top with cinnamon, shaved chocolate, cocoa powder, or powdered sugar….

But first, a question that needs to be addressed: what *exactly* is a cappuccino? First, a cappuccino is *not* a latte! This is one of the most common misconceptions we run across. I think the origin of the misconception is those little convenience store machines that squirt out the milky sweet mixture into a cup and call it cappuccino, or possibly that a frozen drink with a "–uccino" ending is pretty thick. A properly prepared cappuccino is third foam, a third steamed milk, and a third espresso. If a cappuccino is ordered from someone who knows what they're doing, they will ask if you want that wet or dry. Dry is almost all foam, and the cup winds up weighing next to nothing. This delicacy is best had out of a nice china cup, and eaten with a spoon. If the milk is foamed correctly, it has a delectable smooth and rich consistency, making the whole thing not unlike a dessert. Conversely, wet would be about half milk, then espresso, with more foam than a latte but less than a standard cappuccino. And no, cappuccinos can't be made iced. The foamy texture of the milk is lost. So, now that you know exactly what a cappuccino is, lets move on to those delicious lattes!

## *Caramel Nut Latte*

1 oz hazelnut syrup
1 oz caramel syrup
1 shot espresso
1 cup frothed milk
1 dollop fresh whipped cream
Make espresso, froth milk with syrup so syrup doesn't cool your drink, top with whipped cream, and enjoy!

# Caramel Nut Mocha

1 oz chocolate syrup
1 oz caramel syrup
1 oz hazelnut syrup
1 shot espresso
1 cup frothed milk
1 dollop fresh whipped cream
Make espresso, froth milk with syrup so syrup doesn't cool your drink, top with whipped cream, and enjoy!

# Sea Mist Mocha

1 oz white chocolate syrup
1 oz caramel syrup
1 oz hazelnut syrup
1 shot espresso
1 cup frothed milk
1 dollop fresh whipped cream
Make espresso, froth milk with syrup so syrup doesn't cool your drink, top with whipped cream, and enjoy!

# Black Forest Mocha

1 oz chocolate syrup
1 oz black cherry syrup
1 shot espresso
1 cup frothed milk
1 dollop fresh whipped cream
Make espresso, froth milk with syrup so syrup doesn't cool your drink, top with whipped cream, and enjoy!

# Raspberry Fields Forever

1 oz chocolate syrup
1 oz raspberry syrup
1 shot espresso
1 cup frothed milk
1 dollop fresh whipped cream

Make espresso, froth milk with syrup so syrup doesn't cool your drink, top with whipped cream, and enjoy!

## Blond Caramel Nut

1 oz white chocolate syrup
1 oz caramel syrup
1 oz macadamia nut syrup
1 shot espresso
1 cup frothed milk
1 dollop fresh whipped cream
Make espresso, froth milk with syrup so syrup doesn't cool your drink, top with whipped cream, and enjoy!

## White Forest Mocha

1 oz white chocolate syrup
1 oz black cherry syrup
1 shot espresso
1 cup frothed milk
1 dollop fresh whipped cream
Make espresso, froth milk with syrup so syrup doesn't cool your drink, top with whipped cream, and enjoy!

## Double Nothing (AKA Why Bother?)

1 shot decaf espresso
1 cup frothed skim milk
1 dollop fresh whipped cream
Make espresso, froth milk, top with whipped cream, and enjoy!

## Monkey Mocha

1 oz banana syrup
1 oz chocolate syrup
1 shot espresso
1 cup frothed milk
1 dollop fresh whipped cream

Make espresso, froth milk with syrup so syrup doesn't cool your drink, top with whipped cream, and enjoy!

## White Elephant

1 oz white chocolate syrup
1 shot espresso
1 cup frothed milk
1 dollop fresh whipped cream
Make espresso, froth milk with syrup so syrup doesn't cool your drink, top with whipped cream, and enjoy!

## Snickers Mocha

1 oz caramel syrup
1 oz almond syrup
1 oz chocolate syrup
1 shot espresso
1 cup frothed milk
1 dollop fresh whipped cream
Make espresso, froth milk with syrup so syrup doesn't cool your drink, top with whipped cream, and enjoy!

# Chapter Fourteen Iced Coffee Drink Recipes

Iced coffee drinks are best prepared with shots of espresso. Traditionally, iced coffee drinks made at home use regular coffee, but the flavor is so much better with espresso. (It's like the difference between brewed coffee and an Americano.) The drinks can be made in one of two ways, but the most important thing is to have the drink cooled down before the ice is added, so the ice doesn't dilute the drink. There are two ways to do that: use all cold ingredients, or add the cold milk to the hot espresso before adding the ice.

The determining factor is what kinds of syrups you want to add to your drink. For drinks that use a thick chocolate or caramel syrup, you want to use hot espresso to melt the chocolate sauce. For drinks that use just thin flavoring syrups, such as Torani or Monin flavoring syrups, adding to cold espresso is fine, in which case the root of the drink would be the cold espresso you keep in your refrigerator. (See figure 23)

All the drinks in the chapter on frozen drinks can be adapted to being iced drinks, just leave out the frozen latte mix, because it won't dissolve. So, here we go!

## *Iced Coffee*

1 double shot COLD espresso
ice to fill glass

water

Put espresso in glass, fill with cold water (bottled is even better!) and add ice.  Enjoy!

## Iced Mocha

> 1 double shot HOT espresso
> 1 shot chocolate syrup
> 1 cup milk
> ice to fill glass

Mix hot espresso and chocolate syrup together and stir to melt chocolate, add milk to cool mixture, fill with ice.  Enjoy!

## Iced Caramel Nut Mocha

1 double shot HOT espresso
1 shot caramel syrup
1 shot hazelnut flavoring
1 cup milk
ice

Mix hot espresso with caramel syrup, stir to mix.  Add hazelnut flavoring and milk, fill with ice.  Enjoy!

These are the basics, experiment until you find your favorite!

# Chapter Fifteen Blended Coffee Drink Recipes

Blended coffee drinks can also be successfully made at home. Your results will be dramatically improved if you use a commercial grade blender like a Vitamix. The better blenders have better and faster blades that make a more uniform drink that is less likely to have ice chips in it.

The blender drinks will also be better if you use cold espresso, so the ice doesn't melt and water down the drink. The best way to do this is to make 15-20 shots of espresso in advance, and store them in a container in the refrigerator until you are ready to use them. Espresso will stay refrigerated for weeks with no ill effects. A word of warning, though, be sure to cool down the espresso before storing it in a plastic container, or the container will expand and become round from the heat. See figure 23.

Blender drinks come in two basic varieties, drinks with ice cream in them and drinks with plain ice in them. The ice cream drinks use the ice cream to get their volume and texture, and the ice drinks use ice to get their volume and texture. Ice cream drinks can be made just with ice cream, milk, espresso, and flavorings, but the ice drinks will turn out much better if you invest in some powdered latte frozen drink mixes, available at wholesale type stores (Cash N Carry), the internet, and coffee shops. The mix keeps the drink uniform; without it the ice will not mix with the other ingredients and you will wind up with a two part drink.

Figure 23

Some of the best ice cream drinks are made with flavored ice cream. It sounds strange, but it is really good! So, if you want to experiment past the recipes listed here, just get your favorite flavor of ice cream, throw in a shot of espresso, some milk, blend, and enjoy!

A word about the espresso: the best way to make cold espresso drinks is to extract several shots of espresso and refrigerate them. If you use hot espresso, it will melt the ice cream or the ice, and water down the drink. So, get a little plastic or glass container, make 10 or so shots of espresso, and you can leave them in the refrigerator for weeks.

# Coffee Shake

2 oz Kahlua or coffee syrup
1 shot espresso
1 cup milk
1 scoop coffee ice cream
Blend all ingredients until smooth, pour into a tall milkshake glass, enjoy!

# Black Cherry Shake

1 shot espresso
2 oz cherry syrup
1 oz chocolate syrup
I cup milk
1 scoop black cherry ice cream
Blend all ingredients until smooth, enjoy!

# Chocolate Chip Cookie Dough Shake

1 shot espresso
1 oz chocolate syrup
1 cup chocolate cookie dough ice cream
1 cup milk
Blend all ingredients until smooth, pour into a tall milkshake glass, enjoy!

# Chocolate Mocha Brownie Milkshake

1 shot espresso
1 oz chocolate syrup
1 cup chocolate brownie ice cream
1 cup milk
Blend all ingredients until smooth, pour into a tall milkshake glass, enjoy!

# Frozen Black Forest

1 shot espresso

1 shot cherry syrup
1 oz chocolate syrup
1 scoop frozen latte mix
1 cup milk
1 cup ice
Blend all ingredients until smooth, pour into a tall milkshake glass, enjoy!

## Frozen Caramel Nut

1 oz caramel sauce
1 shot espresso
1 shot nut flavored syrup
1 scoop frozen latte mix
1 cup milk
1 cup ice
Blend all ingredients until smooth, pour into a tall milkshake glass, enjoy!

## Peppermint Patty Milkshake

1 shot espresso
1 oz chocolate syrup
1 cup mint chocolate chip ice cream
1 cup milk
Blend all ingredients until smooth, pour into a tall milkshake glass, enjoy!

## Banana Chocolate Cooler

1/2 ripe banana
1/2 cup chocolate frozen yogurt or ice cream
1/2 cup strong cold brewed coffee
1/2 cup ice cubes
Blend until smooth, enjoy!

## Food Processor Truffles

1/2 lb semisweet chocolate chips

1/2 cup strong brewed coffee
1 tbs butter
1 tbs liqueur of your choice (Chambord is fun!)
1/2 cup unsweetened cocoa

Using the steel blade of a food processor, chop the chocolate very fine. Heat coffee until just below boiling, add coffee to feed tube with machine running. Add butter and liqueur and scrape sides of the work bowl. Continue processing until well combined and smooth. Chill until firm enough to be shaped. Form into small balls using a melon scoop, a teaspoon or your hands. Roll in cocoa. Store in a covered container well sealed in the 'fridge for up to 2 weeks. May be frozen for up to 3 months.

# Chapter Sixteen After Dinner Coffee Drink Recipes

The combination of good after-dinner coffee with a dash of liquor and a dollop of whipped cream is one of life's simple pleasures! Instead of the usual Irish Coffee, try one of these recipes for your next after-dinner drink! Sprinkle a little cinnamon or cocoa powder on top of the whipped cream, and if you're really feeling adventurous, make homemade whipped cream for your drink! Just put heavy whipping cream in a food processor and run until the cream thickens. Or, use a bowl and wire whip. Just make sure you don't over-process, or you'll wind up with butter!

(If you do over-process the cream, go for the butter instead of throwing it out. Finish running until the butter is in clumps in a bath of milk, put the clumps in a small bowl, press with a spatula until all the milky liquid comes out, and viola, you've got fresh butter! It won't have the several week long shelf life that regular butter has, because you'll never be able to get all the milky liquid out, but it will last for a week and be excellent. Actually, while you're at it, you could use it to make compound butters, where you add some garlic powder, onion powder, and snipped fresh chives, and use on fresh bread at dinner. Or, for fun breakfast butter, add some cinnamon, sugar, and nutmeg, and use on French Toast or regular toast.)

Even whipped creams have come a long way, baby! Add sugar for sweeter whipped cream. Accent your whipped cream with a little vanilla. Splash a little Chambord in your whipped cream, or use some chocolate syrup or caramel syrup!  The only trick is to get the cream whipped up before you accent it with other flavors.

## Mocha Double

1 oz Kahlua
1 oz Crème de cacao
top with freshly brewed coffee
and a dollop of whipped cream

## Orange Swirl

1 oz Tuaca
1 oz Grand Marnier
top with freshly brewed coffee
and a dollop of whipped cream

## Mexican Coffee

1 oz Kahlua
1 oz Frangelico
Sprinkle of cinnamon
top with freshly brewed coffee
and a dollop of whipped cream

## Love at First Sip

1 oz Amaretto De Amore
1 oz brandy
top with freshly brewed coffee
and a dollop of whipped cream

## Orange Burst

1 oz cognac
1 oz Grand Marnier
top with freshly brewed coffee
and a dollop of whipped cream

# Luck O' the Irish

1 oz Bailey's Irish Crème
1 oz Frangelico
1 oz Irish Whiskey
top with freshly brewed coffee
and a dollop of whipped cream

# Chocolate Orange Coffee

1 oz Grand Marnier
1 oz Dark Cacao
1 oz Tia Maria
top with freshly brewed coffee
and a dollop of whipped cream

# Monk's Coffee

1 oz Bailey's Irish Crème
1 oz Frangelico
top with freshly brewed coffee
and a dollop of whipped cream

# Chocolate Kicker

1 oz Kahlua
1 oz Dark Cacao
1 oz. Brandy
top with freshly brewed coffee
and a dollop of whipped cream

# Tropical Coffee

1 oz Myers Rum
1 oz Tia Maria
top with freshly brewed coffee
and a dollop of whipped cream

# Orange Firestorm Coffee

1 oz Bacardi 151 rum
1 oz Kahlua
1 oz Triple Sec
top with freshly brewed coffee
and a dollop of whipped cream

## *Sweet Finish Coffee*

1 oz Tia Maria
1 oz Bailey's Irish Cream
top with freshly brewed coffee
and a dollop of whipped cream

## *Raspberry Magic*

1 oz Chambord
1 oz raspberry syrup
top with freshly brewed coffee
and a dollop of whipped cream!

# Chapter Seventeen Food Recipes

These are some of our favorite recipes, all accented with coffee! The instructions have the reason why something is prepared a certain way. It drives us nuts to read a recipe in a cookbook and have them say "but whatever you do, don't do X" and then not tell us what happens if you do "X" which only makes us want to do what they said not to do, just to see what happens! So, we've tried to give the reason for steps to avoid, to satisfy your curiosity!

Warning: None of these are diet foods! Although, even the idea of dieting has recently been revamped! If you're on one of those low carbohydrate diets, some of these recipes, like the BBQ Ribs, would be pretty good! Just cut back a little on the brown sugar, or use one of those brown sugar substitutes. The coffee adds a mysterious rich flavor that can't be discerned as coffee, but definitely contributes to the overall dish!

A few of these recipes call for chipotle or ancho chilis. Most larger grocery stores carry these items in either the spice section or the Mexican foods section, so you should have no trouble finding them, or check out the internet. If you still can't find 'em, visit us online at www.villageroastery.com, and use the link to send an email, and we'll ship you some. We've got lots.

# *Mocha Scones*

You can make scones at home that are every bit as good as the scones you buy out, and they are a lot less expensive made at home, too! To get really great scones, there are a few things you need to keep in mind. First, don't overwork the dough. Once the dough is mixed, gluten starts to develop from the flour, which is great if you're making bread, but is extremely undesirable if you're making scones, because it will make them tough. So, mix a few strokes, move dough to the board, press out, and cut into pieces.

The other thing to watch for is putting sugar on the baking sheet instead of flour. It seems like a really great idea, but what will happen is the sugar will burn at the high temperatures necessary to cook scones. Sprinkle the sugar on the top, and leave the baking sheet plain or lightly greased. Here's the recipe:

2 cups flour

1/3 cup sugar

1 T baking powder

1¾ cup cream

2 T espresso

1 c chocolate chips

1 T raw sugar for garnish

Mix the flour, sugar, and baking powder until blended. Add the espresso to the cream. Add cream mixture to flour mixture all at once, and stir and mix just until blended (about 5-10 seconds). Transfer to a cutting board. Flatten out the dough and put the chocolate chips on top. Fold over the dough to cover the chips, and press down very lightly. Form the dough into a circle, about 10" round and 1" thick. Don't overwork the dough, somewhere near round is good enough! The chips should be inside the dough. Sprinkle some sugar on the top and press in slightly. Cut into pie shaped wedges. If any of the chips fall out, just press them back into the dough. You want the chips to be mostly covered by the dough, otherwise they will burn. Preheat oven to 400°, bake on lightly greased cookie sheet for 10 minutes. Remove to rack to cool. Enjoy with a latte or cappuccino!

# BBQ Pork Ribs

2-4 lbs Baby Back Ribs
1 cup strong coffee
1½ cups catsup
4 T Worcestershire Sauce
½ cup brown sugar
¼ cup cider vinegar
1 t garlic powder
1 t chili powder
½ cup ancho chili puree

These are absolutely delish! If you're into Baby Back Pork Ribs, these are the finest you will ever try! The secret is in the preparation, and the sauce becomes the "icing on the cake" if you will!

Take the rack of ribs, and pre-portion them into six or seven (or eight or nine!) ribs per portion. This will help them fit into the cooking pot. Otherwise, you have a 3 foot long strip of ribs, which besides being unwieldy, will not cook evenly.

Next, trim off the visible fat clumps. Simmer the ribs in water on the stove for 10 minutes or so, just enough to get the rest of the obvious fat off. Now for the big secret: put the ribs in a Dutch oven, add about one inch of water, cover the ribs tightly, and put in a 250° oven for 3 hours.

Meanwhile, make the sauce by mixing the ingredients in a saucepan and simmering slowly, being careful not to let it burn.

Check the ribs during the last hour of cooking, and when they have shrunk back from the bones slightly test them with a fork. The meat should literally fall from the bones. If it doesn't put 'em back in for another half hour and check again. When the ribs are so tender you just want to take them out and eat them right then, remove from the oven and turn the oven up to 325. Lay the ribs out in single layer on a baking sheet, and slather with the BBQ sauce. Bake until the sauce has heated through and is kind of glazed (you'll know it when you see it) but not burned, remove from oven, and you've got the best ribs in the world! Serve with extra sauce on the side for dipping, High-test BBQ Baked Beans, and lots of cold beer! YUM!

# *High-Test BBQ Baked Beans*

2 cans baked beans
½ lb honey cured bacon
1 large onion
½ cup ancho chili puree*
1 T Chipotle chili en adobe**
½ cup molasses
¼ cup catsup
½ cup brown sugar
2 T Dijon style mustard

Cut bacon into small pieces, and sauté with diced onions until soft. Don't let it burn! Drain off excess fat. Combine with the rest of the ingredients and bake at 350° for 45 minutes or until bubbly.

*ancho chilies can be bought in their dried form in most Mexican stores, and good sized regular grocery stores. To rehydrate them, just break them open to expose the inside (this greatly reduces cooking time), boil in water until you can see that the skins have plumped up (this takes maybe 10-15 minutes), puree in a food processor, and strain. Save the rest in your refrigerator, and use for Mexican foods.

**these are those little cans of chipotles available in almost every grocery store in little 7 oz tins. They contain viciously hot chipotles (Smoked jalapenos, for those of you who didn't already know) in a thick tomato-like sauce. To be successfully used, puree the whole can and then save the rest in a small glass jar in the refrigerator. If you don't puree them before you use them, you've only got one or two very large, very hot chipotles (smoked jalapenos, remember), and whomever gets a whole jalapeno in one bite of beans will swear vengeance on you and your progeny for all time! Anyway, store the rest in the refrigerator, and next time you're eating Mexican food, mix a little with some sour cream and use it as an excellent garnish!

# *Chocolate Espresso Tart*

This is one of those totally decadent recipes! Don't even think about the calories in this one!

For the Crust:

2 ¼ cups flour

½ cup slivered almonds

¼ cup sugar

1 ½ sticks butter

1 egg

Process the slivered almonds in a food processor, add the flour, sugar, and butter, and process until it turns into large crumbs. Add the egg, and mix by hand until it forms smooth dough. Knead a few times until it comes together and roll out carefully, being careful not to overwork the dough (which will make it tough). Transfer to a large pie pan or spring form pan, and bake for until it's light brown, about 20 minutes at 350°.

For the filling:

2 eggs

6 egg yolks

¼ cup sugar

12 oz bittersweet or other dark chocolate

1 ½ T espresso

2 sticks butter

Mix together the eggs, egg yolks and sugar until smooth. Melt the chocolate and butter together. Don't add the espresso until the chocolate has been melted and blended with the butter, or the chocolate will turn grainy. Cool slightly, add the espresso, add half the chocolate mix to the egg mixture, and mix together. Add this back into the balance of the egg mixture, pour into the crust, and finish in the oven at 400° for 15 minutes. It won't look done, but it is. Remove and cool, garnish with sliced strawberries and whipped cream, and serve. Yum! Then don't weigh yourself for a week!

## *Chocolate Espresso Cheesecake*

If you want to make a really excellent cheesecake, go to a restaurant supply house and buy a professional cheesecake spring form pan. They are 3 to 3.5 inches tall, and make a much better cheesecake than the 2-inch tall supermarket pans. A secret to not getting lumpy batter is to process the cream cheese thoroughly until smooth *prior* to adding liquid ingredients like eggs, which thin the batter too much and leave lumps of cream cheese.

For the crust:

2/3 of a 15 oz package of Oreo cookies (2 rows)

2 T sugar

½ stick melted butter

Process Oreo cookies in food processor until broken into small pieces. You may need to stop and manually crush some of the cookies if they don't break up, then run again. Add 2T sugar and blend, then add ½ stick *melted* butter while the processor is running, and blend just until mixed. Be sure that the butter is thoroughly mixed with the cookie mixture. Pour mix into greased springform pan, and press against edges with the back of a large metal spoon. (wood spoons don't work well for this) Tipping the pan on a 45-degree angle and pressing down while rotating the pan is the best way to do this. Feather the crust so it's thick at the bottom of the pan and thins out near the top. If you don't, it will fall back into the pan and be amazingly frustrating. Then manually press the rest of the mix into the bottom of the pan. Don't press too hard, or the crust will be too hard. Just press enough to keep the mix where you put it, without compressing it. If the crust isn't as thick as you'd like, make the last third package of Oreos into a little more crust.

For the filling:

3ea 8oz boxes cream cheese

½ cup sugar

1 cup sour cream

2 eggs

4 heaping T good quality cocoa

1 T Vanilla

1 shot espresso  (2 T)

Mix cream cheese in food processor until smooth. Scrape down the sides and mix again. If you skip this step, your batter will be lumpy. Add sugar and process again until smooth. Scrape down bowl again and blend until smooth. Add eggs and sour cream, process until smooth. Divide the batter in half. Add the espresso to half the batter, and add the cocoa powder to the other half. Add the vanilla to the cocoa half of the batter. Pour the chocolate batter into the springform, and then pour the espresso mix on top. Being very careful not to hit the crust, use a spoon to lift up the bottom half and swirl into the top half. (If you hit the crust, you'll bring up pieces of the cookie crust into the cheesecake, which won't hurt anything, but won't look as pretty.) When you're done, you should have a nice swirl pattern on the top.

Bake at 350° for about an hour, until when you tap the side of the pan the cheesecake all moves together. (Before it's done, when you tap it the outside will move and the center will not.) It won't look done, but pull it out anyway. Let it cool, preferably overnight. Once it's cool, slice and enjoy! Top with homemade whipped cream and strawberry slices. If you are worried about eating (or not eating!) all the rest, carefully wrap in several layers of Saran wrap or put in a freezer bag, and freeze for up to one month. If it is late one night and you've got the munchies for cheesecake, get out the frozen cheesecake, slice off a big slab with a large chef knife (being careful of your fingers) and pop into the microwave for about a minute to thaw and warm. Slightly warm cheesecake is actually pretty good! Especially if you drown it in hot chocolate sauce! A perfect late night snack!

# Chapter Eighteen Something for Tea Lovers, too!

Tea, being an agricultural product, has varying grades and degrees of quality, just like coffee, wine grapes, and everything else that grows. These differences in turn affect the taste and appearance of the final product. Long, smooth, perfectly formed soft tea leaves from the top of the plant are obviously going to command a higher price than the ground up dust left from processing the bottom stalks and tough leaves closer to the ground.

Tea comes in two basic forms: green tea and black tea. Halfway in-between is Oolong tea. Figure 24 shows, clockwise from upper left, what's inside a teabag, black tea, green tea, and oolong tea. The difference between green tea and black tea is the processing it undergoes. Green tea is unfermented, black tea is fermented, and Oolong tea is in-between, or partially fermented. Green tea tends to be milder, with lower caffeine, and black tea is definitely stronger, with higher caffeine. Black tea makes much better iced tea than green tea does. No matter how long you leave green tea leaves in the water, it just won't make a tea strong enough to ice.

When the tea is processed, there are long top leafs with the bud included, which is the most prized. After that is long leaf tea, then broken leafs, then dust, which is mostly used in tea bags. Interestingly enough, dust yields a much stronger cup of tea, probably because of the increased surface area. But for taste, the long leaves can't be beat! Dust imparts a bitter taste to tea, whereas tea made from the top leaves has a smooth flavor.

Figure 24

Tea ranges in quality just like coffee and wine, and prices are commensurate with quality. Top of the line green tea costs upwards of $600.00 a pound! The best tea estates yield the best tea, just like wine and coffee, and as the quality goes down, the identity fades until it winds up in tea bags that yield an almost unpalatably astringent drink.

Once tea is processed, it can be flavored in several ways. The most famous flavored tea of them all, Earl Grey, is a base tea with Oil of Bergamot added. The base tea can be of any different grade, and the Oil of Bergamot can be any of several different grades. This results in many different grades of Earl Grey, with tastes and flavors ranging from store bought Earl Grey tea bags to the finest of Assam teas flavored with the finest Oil of Bergamot, available only in specialty tea shops and commanding prices upwards of $50.00 per pound.

Teas can be flavored with syrups, just like coffee, and they can also be flavored with the addition of other ingredients, spices, and plant components. For example, Cherry Sencha is a green sencha tea with cherry blossoms added, and Rose Sencha has rose hips and petals added to the tea. Both black and green teas can be flavored, although semi-fermented Oolongs are rarely flavored. Black flavored teas make delicious iced teas, too, but green flavored teas just don't get strong enough.

Another wildly popular flavored tea is Chai, which is made by boiling tea with spices like cardamom, cinnamon and ginger, then adding milk and boiling again. Although Chai tea in coffee shops is usually made by heating a mix, authentic Chai tea is made by boiling tea (I know, treason to boil tea!) with spices and adding the milk.

Then there are the herbals. Herbal teas can be made with a base plant that is used as a tea substitute, such as Yerba Mate and African Rooibos, both caffeine free plants that resemble tea in appearance, or herbal teas can be made as combinations of herbs, flowers and mints.

To get the best results from tea, the proper brewing method must be used. Different types of teas require different water temperatures and steeping times, and the tea must be removed from the water after steeping to prevent bitterness. Some green tea leaves can be used again after the first time, although there will be a marked reduction in flavor.

## *How tea is graded:*

Tea is graded with some similarities to coffee. Remember, coffee is graded by the quality of the bean and the size of the bean. Tea is graded by the quality of the leaf and the size of the leaf.

The quality of the leaf has to do with where on the plant the leaf was grown. The finest teas are comprised of the handpicked top two leaves and the bud. The bottom of the scale is when the rest of the plant is mechanically harvested to get all the remaining leaves. There isn't much in-between, except for how many of the leaves become broken during processing.

Then the tea is graded according to size. There is invariably some damage to the leaves when the tea is picked, when it is processed, and when it is packed. The meticulously perfect top two leafs and bud command the highest price when they are whole. I personally have paid $198.00/lb for green gunpowder tea that when brewed unfolds perfectly into two perfect leaves and the bud. (If you'd like some, send me an email!) This is really special occasion tea!

Then comes the broken leaf tea, then what's known as fannings, and lastly (and **least**!) is the dust. The dust is reserved for use in tea bags, and although the flavor is generally somewhat substandard, this is one of the strongest forms of tea, because of all the surface area exposed to the water for infusion.

After tea has been graded, it is cupped much like coffee to determine its flavor characteristics. Defects range from grassy to bitter, and are easily distinguished both by taste and smell. And, like coffee, a lot of defects are introduced in the production and processing.

## *The Grades:*

Whole Leaf
Broken Leaf
Fannings
Dust

The Subsets:

## **Whole Leaf**

***SFTGFOP-- Special Finest Tippy Golden Flowery Orange Pekoe*** - This grade is primarily used to grade Darjeeling teas with a large proportion of leaves having golden tips on new leaf buds. A guarantee of quality.

***FTGFOP -- Finest Tippy Golden Flowery Orange Pekoe -*** Another grade primarily used to grade Indian black teas consisting of Exceptional quality *OP* with lots of tips.

***TGFOP-- Tippy Golden Flowery Orange Pekoe -OP*** with a lower proportion tips.

***OP-- Orange Pekoe -*** Long, pointed leaves that are harvested when the terminal buds open into leaf. Rarely contains *"tips"*.

***GFOP --Golden Flowery Orange Pekoe -FOP*** with a certain amount of golden tips.

*FP --Flowery Pekoe -*
Shorter, Coarser leaves. The next leaves down *OP*.
*PS -- Pekoe Souchong -*Pekoe leaf further broken down is Pekoe
Souchong.
*Souchong--*Shorter and tightly rolled leaf style (for Indian
Souchong). But when used for grading Chinese teas this refers to
large leaves.
*Pouchong--*A variety of tea that is very rare. The leaf is extra large
and when brewed the infused leaf extends to at least an inch and a
half in length.

## Broken Leaf Tea

*GFBOP --Golden Flowery Broken Orange Pekoe*
*FBOP-- Flowery Broken Orange Pekoe*
*GBOP-- Golden Broken Orange Pekoe*
*TGBOP-- Tippy Golden Broken Orange Pekoe*
*BOP-- Broken Orange Pekoe*

## Fannings

*» Broken Orange Pekoe Fannings - BOPF*
Leaf size is smaller than *BOP* is grade as fannings. This grade is
primarily used in tea bags since it brews very quickly and its size is
small.

## Dust

The leaf size smaller than *BOPF* is graded as Dust. Dust grades
brew an extra strong cup and are popular with caterers and are also
used in tea bags.

*Nancy Faubel*

# *Reasons to Drink Tea*

- It's natural, pure and safe to drink
- It's free of fat, carbohydrates, and chemicals
- It's refreshing and relaxing
- It improves longevity
- It brings friends closer together
- It reduces cholesterol
- It's high in antioxidants
- It's low in caffeine
- It stimulates thinking
- It overcomes drowsiness
- It tastes good
- It's good value!

# *Some Tea Terminology*

The criteria used for including a word or expression in this list was that it had to be something we'd found that people were unsure of.

**Black Tea-Regular**-fermented tea from tea-producing regions from around the world

**Black Tea-Flavored**-Nilgiri tea from India, accented with various fruits and spices.

**Green Tea**-Unfermented tea from tea producing regions around the world

**Green Sencha**-an exquisite flat leaf Japanese tea

**Green Gunpowder**: called this because the hand rolled leaves resemble gunpowder. Available in many forms, from pinhead gunpowder which is very small, to very large tea balls approaching an inch in diameter.

**English breakfast**-a mild combination of unflavored balck teas such as Assam and Ceylon teas.

**Irish Breakfast** slightly stronger than English breakfast, made so by a subtle difference in the ratio of the blend, and using teas from different origins. Always black tea, though.

**Jasmine** a usually green tea infused with the essence of jasmine flowers, a perennial flavor favorite.

**Genmaicha**-green Japanese Sencha accented with rice and popped corn. Sounds strange, but really good!

**Indian masala chai**-a black tea prepared by boiling tea and spices together, then adding milk. A traditional tea in India. A good chai tea will contain all the authentic chai ingredients of cinnamon cardamom, cloves, etc, but without all the added sugar, so you can sweeten to taste.

**Darjeeling**-often referred to as the champagne of teas, Darjeeling is from the finest Indian tea estates of the Darjeeling area of India.

**Lapsang Souchong**-a smoky flavored tea produced by smoking the leaves as they dry. Interesting and very different.

**Oolong** a semi fermented tea.

**Herbals and caffeine free**-yerba mate and African rooibos are two types, made from plants other than tea, and naturally caffeine free.

# Chapter Nineteen Tea Cupping Worksheets

Use the worksheets to compare your favorite teas. Filling out the worksheets will help you notice things about different teas that you might otherwise not have noticed, like the difference in fragrance, the difference in color, and the difference in aroma. Comparing teas side by side is an excellent way to really see the differences between them, and it helps develop your palate and appreciation, too!

## Tea Cupping Worksheet

Instructions: Note type of tea in top row, grade each characteristic. Keep for future reference for tea purchases.

| Type of Tea/ Region | | | | | | | | |
|---|---|---|---|---|---|---|---|---|
| Leaf Appearance (Tip) | | | | | | | | |
| Liquor (Brewed color) | | | | | | | | |
| Clarity | | | | | | | | |
| Brightness | | | | | | | | |
| General appearance Coppery/bright | | | | | | | | |
| Aroma/ nose Smoky/sweet | | | | | | | | |
| Taste Clean/brisk Flat/dull | | | | | | | | |
| Notes/ Remarks | | | | | | | | |

## Tea Cupping Worksheet

Instructions: Note type of tea in top row, grade each characteristic. keep for future reference for tea purchases.

| Type of Tea/ Region | | | | | | | | |
|---|---|---|---|---|---|---|---|---|
| Leaf Appearance (Tip) | | | | | | | | |
| Liquor (Brewed color) | | | | | | | | |
| Clarity | | | | | | | | |
| Brightness | | | | | | | | |
| General appearance Coppery/bright | | | | | | | | |
| Aroma/ nose Smoky/sweet | | | | | | | | |
| Taste Clean/brisk Flat/dull | | | | | | | | |
| Notes/ Remarks | | | | | | | | |

## Tea Cupping Worksheet

Instructions: Note type of tea in top row, grade each characteristic. keep for future reference for tea purchases.

| | | | | | | | | |
|---|---|---|---|---|---|---|---|---|
| **Type of Tea/Region** | | | | | | | | |
| **Leaf Appearance (Tip)** | | | | | | | | |
| **Liquor (Brewed color)** | | | | | | | | |
| **Clarity** | | | | | | | | |
| **Brightness** | | | | | | | | |
| **General appearance** Coppery/bright | | | | | | | | |
| **Aroma/nose** Smoky/sweet | | | | | | | | |
| **Taste** Clean/brisk Flat/dull | | | | | | | | |
| **Notes/Remarks** | | | | | | | | |

89

# Chapter Twenty Coffee Cupping Worksheets

The process for cupping coffee was covered in detail in an earlier chapter; here are the worksheets for tallying your final results. At first, it will be hard, because the first sip of the first coffee, you won't really know if it's full bodied or high/low acidity or whatever. But, as you continue cupping, and continue comparing, the differences become easier and easier to distinguish, and pretty soon you'll know a full bodied coffee instantly, without having to compare it to another coffee, and you'll know a high acidity coffee (remember, it tastes like sparkling water) from a low acidity coffee (remember, it tastes like tap water) immediately! So, keep up the good work, and remember, it will refine and hone your taste for coffee, and really help you decide which is your favorite, and which you'd rather pass on!

And remember, keep your notes, and eventually, you'll be able to detect differences from season to season and even from crop to crop!

# Coffee Cupping Worksheet

## The Coffee

| Country | Region | Estate | Cost | Score |
|---------|--------|--------|------|-------|
|         |        |        |      |       |

## The Bean

**Bean Size:**    15    16    17    18    19    Peaberry    Other

**Cultivar:**    Bourbon    Typica    Longberry    Maragogype    Caturra    Other

**Grade:**    1    2    3    4    5    A    AA    AAA    Xfancy    High-Grown    SHB    SHG    Other

**Processed:**          Dry (Yellow/Green)          Wet (Blue/Green)          Semi-washed

**Roast:**    Medium-Light          Medium          Medium Dark          Dark          Very Dark

## The Taste

**Fragrance:** (smell of coffee before adding water– indicates the roast)

**Aroma:** (smell of coffee after adding water–indicates flavor and brightness)

**Flavor** (Overall Taste)

**Acidity** (Brightness and dryness)

**Body** (Weight of coffee (press tongue against roof of mouth), indicates oil content)

**Aftertaste** (Permanence of initial aromatic sensation)

## The Score

| Fragrance | Aroma | Flavor | Acidity | Body | Aftertaste | Total |
|-----------|-------|--------|---------|------|------------|-------|
| -3 to +3 | -3 to +3 | 1 to 10 | 1 to 10 | 1 to 10 | 1 to 10 | Sum |
|           |        |         |         |      |            |       |

## Coffee Cupping Worksheet

### The Coffee

| Country | Region | Estate | Cost | Score |
|---------|--------|--------|------|-------|
|         |        |        |      |       |

### The Bean

**Bean Size:**   15   16   17   18   19   Peaberry   Other

**Cultivar:**   Bourbon   Typica   Longberry   Maragogype   Caturra   Other

**Grade:**   1  2  3  4  5  A  AA  AAA  Xfancy  High-Grown  SHB  SHG Other

**Processed:**        Dry (Yellow/Green)        Wet (Blue/Green)    Semi-washed

**Roast:**   Medium-Light      Medium      Medium Dark    Dark    Very Dark

### The Taste

**Fragrance:** (smell of coffee before adding water– indicates the roast)

**Aroma:** (smell of coffee after adding water-indicates flavor and brightness)

**Flavor** (Overall Taste)

**Acidity** (Brightness and dryness)

**Body** (Weight of coffee (press tongue against roof of mouth), indicates oil content)

**Aftertaste** (Permanence of initial aromatic sensation)

### The Score

| Fragrance | Aroma | Flavor | Acidity | Body | Aftertaste | Total |
|-----------|-------|--------|---------|------|-----------|-------|
| -3 to +3  | -3 to +3 | 1 to 10 | 1 to 10 | 1 to 10 | 1 to 10 | Sum |
|           |       |        |         |      |           |       |

# Coffee Cupping Worksheet

## The Coffee

| Country | Region | Estate | Cost | Score |
|---|---|---|---|---|
| | | | | |

## The Bean

**Bean Size:**  15   16   17   18   19   Peaberry   Other

**Cultivar:**  Bourbon   Typica   Longberry   Maragogype   Caturra   Other

**Grade:**  1  2  3  4  5  A  AA  AAA  Xfancy  High-Grown  SHB  SHG  Other

**Processed:**  Dry (Yellow/Green)   Wet (Blue/Green)   Semi-washed

**Roast:**  Medium-Light   Medium   Medium Dark   Dark   Very Dark

## The Taste

**Fragrance:** (smell of coffee before adding water– indicates the roast)

**Aroma:** (smell of coffee after adding water-indicates flavor and brightness)

**Flavor** (Overall Taste)

**Acidity** (Brightness and dryness)

**Body** (Weight of coffee (press tongue against roof of mouth), indicates oil content)

**Aftertaste** (Permanence of initial aromatic sensation)

## The Score

| Fragrance | Aroma | Flavor | Acidity | Body | Aftertaste | Total |
|---|---|---|---|---|---|---|
| -3 to +3 | -3 to +3 | 1 to 10 | 1 to 10 | 1 to 10 | 1 to 10 | Sum |
| | | | | | | |

# Chapter Twenty-One Sources

Most of the ingredient listed in this book should be able to be purchased locally. If you have difficulty finding any of the ingredients listed in this book, check out our website at:

www.villageroastery.com

or contact us at :

The Village Roastery

PO Box 1691

Winchester Bay, OR 97467

Phone

541-271-3424

Fax

541-271-3422

# About The Author

Nancy C. Faubel has been involved in the world of gourmet coffee since 1998, when she first learned how to roast specialty coffee and prepare espresso in the Italian style. She owns The Village Roastery in Winchester Bay, Oregon, and distributes coffee throughout the United States, Canada, Alaska, and Hawaii. Prior to her entry into the world of coffee, she owned the largest FAA-approved Flight School in North Carolina and offered all pilot ratings up to Airline Transport Pilot-Multiengine.

Ms. Faubel was born in Rochester, New York, and received a BS degree in Engineering from Alfred University and an MBA from the University of Rochester. Her hobbies include aviation, fused glass art, gourmet cooking, writing, travel, and golf.

Printed in the United States
130665LV00001B/179/A